SCUBA PROFESSIONAL

Insights into Sport Diver Training & Operations

SIMON PRIDMORE

Sandsmedia Publishing
BALI, INDONESIA

Sandsmedia Publishing, Bali, Indonesia 80363

www.scubaconfidential.com

Book Layout ©2015 Createspace.com and Sandsmedia

Cover Image by Andrey Bizyukin

Scuba Professional/Simon Pridmore. 1st ed.

ISBN-13: 978-1507621073

ISBN-10: 1507621078

For Sofie,
eternal muse and demanding editor

The Expert View

There is quite simply nothing like this book. If you are considering becoming a diving professional or want to improve your skills and marketability as one, this is the best resource you will find. Written by an experienced and thoughtful professional with countless unique experiences within varied aspects of the industry, Scuba Professional offers an invaluable guide to divers who want to excel in the scuba world. Cautionary tales, thoughtful anecdotes and sage advice are interlaced with great insight into the inner workings of the diving industry. Simon Pridmore's book is the ultimate backstage pass into the business of scuba.

Jill Heinerth, Underwater Explorer, Technical Instructor Trainer and Filmmaker

Terrific, really good! Simon captures the key characteristics of the diving instruction milieu concisely and with insight and clarity. It took me back to my many years of diving instruction and I was able to tick a mental check box against almost every key point he makes. This book should be compulsory reading for anyone in training, or contemplating training, as a diving instructor. Established instructors will find themselves nodding in agreement, and will inevitably pick up a pearl or two.

Associate Professor Simon Mitchell, MB ChB, PhD, DipDHM, DipOccMed, FUHM, FANZCA, Consultant Anaesthetist and Diving Physician

Just as he did in his previous book, the cult classic *Scuba Confidential: An Insider's Guide to Becoming a Better Diver*, author, educator and technical diving pioneer Simon Pridmore has distilled more than three decades of diving experience, wisdom and culture into *Scuba Professional,* his thoughtful and entertaining new treatise.

Pridmore's book is a must-read for instructors, operators, other dive professionals and anyone considering making a career out of diving. The book is filled with invaluable insights, tips, incidents and anecdotes and also addresses timely and critical topics such as creating a safety culture in diving, developing sustainable dive tourism, applying rebreather technology to recreational diving and the future development of the sport. His clear, comfortable writing style makes it an engaging read. I recommend that you do!

Michael Menduno, founder of aquaCORPS Journal, the tek.Conference, EuroTek, AsiaTek and Rebreather Forums.

Required reading for every scuba professional and anyone with hopes of becoming one. In fact every diver can learn from this distillation of hard-earned wisdom. Simon Pridmore is one of the most thoughtful and readable of divers.

Steve Weinman, Editor, Diver Magazine

Simon Pridmore's Scuba Professional is packed with anecdotes from a life spent pursuing the passion of scuba diving. Many dream of turning this passion into a rewarding career and the key to making the transition successfully lies in these pages. Dive professionals will find many suggestions for improvement here. I wish this book had been available 20 years ago!

Tamara Thomsen, Maritime Archaeologist, Wisconsin Historical Society; Master Instructor, Cave Instructor and owner Diversions Scuba, Madison, Wisconsin

Table of Contents

Foreword

N ow what? You have passed your course and achieved the long coveted certification as a dive master or instructor. Perhaps you have already been a dive professional for a while. In any case you are now considering going all in and make diving your next career move.

Moving up the certification ladder has, one would hope, made you a proficient and experienced diver and provided you with a range of teaching skills, tools and techniques to enable you to train new cohorts of aspiring divers safely and consistently in compliance with international standards. So you have got your basics covered.

Alas, you have only the basics. There is so much more to it. Becoming an instructor is probably the most common gateway into becoming a dive industry professional. But it is only a starting point.

Being a dive industry professional is not a clearly defined entity let alone a formal job description. It is a rather diffuse term that can be attributed to anyone who predominantly makes a living in the dive industry. There are no pre-set career paths, no formal training requirements and certainly no such thing as a dive industry academy offering further education in this particular field.

The dive industry can be thought of as a messy meritocracy, where a wide range of quite different skills are required and put to use -and where entrepreneurship, improvisation and tenancy are often key for any long-term tenure.

By dissecting and laying out the inner workings of this seething and ever changing marketplace, Simon Pridmore has managed to put no small measure of meaning to the madness, pointing out viable niches, going over success stories and mapping out possible pathways through the chaos, some of which have already been trodden by first venturers. He points out footsteps that can be followed, cites case histories to use for inspiration and shares hard-learned mistakes to take to heart.

As such, "Scuba Professional" is the closest thing we have to an 'insiders guide to the dive industry.' It should be perused by anyone who has aspirations for a career in diving and is seeking guidance. Or it can just be read as an entertaining behind-the-scenes documentary highlighting many of the diverse, multi-facetted and colourful aspects of the dive industry and its captivating personalities with their often intriguing and twisty career paths. There is never a dull moment in this industry and you won't have one either when you read this book.

Peter Symes, Editor-in-chief and publisher of X-Ray International Magazine & AquaScope Media

Preface

A couple of years ago, while I was writing my first book, more than a few people told me I was wasting my time." "Divers don't even read their training manuals," they said. However, with a ton of ideas on my mind, I ignored their advice and fortunately they were wrong. The success of Scuba Confidential proves that divers do read! Emboldened, I decided to write another book, this time with a more experienced audience in mind.

Scuba Professional is mainly for three groups of people. First it is for folk I would call serious divers. What do I mean by serious divers? I mean people for whom scuba diving is a large part of their life. They are interested in far more than simply going underwater: they are also curious to know how the world of scuba diving works. And rightly so: after all, although their involvement in scuba diving may be mainly as customers, their opinions, choices, input and enthusiasm have a huge influence on the dive industry.

Scuba Professional is also for anyone thinking of making a career in the sport. Working in scuba diving can be highly rewarding but it takes much dedication and a certain amount of political nous to make a success of it. Many people come into the sport professionally with their eyes half-closed and it takes them a while before they realise what they have got themselves into. Scuba Professional aims to give potential recruits a clear idea of what is involved and help them make the right decisions.

This book is, of course, also written for current professionals. There are very few resources out there that dive centre managers and instructors can consult on matters relating to teaching scuba diving or running dive operations. Most of the material available is training agency – sponsored so it is primarily sales driven and designed to reinforce an agency's particular way of doing things. Scuba Professional is different in that it raises a whole host of important issues that affect dive professionals everywhere and discusses them with common sense, straight talking and no hidden agenda.

Safety Culture

Both my books embrace the concept of developing a stronger safety culture in diving. Where Scuba Confidential addressed dive safety issues from the perspective of the diver as an individual, Scuba Professional takes a wider view, looking at how dive operations and instructors can implement best practices. Everyone in the industry will always claim that safety is their primary consideration but the fact of the matter is that, for many, this is patently not the case. Sometimes, financial considerations, fatigue or apathy intrude. This is not as it should be. A key premise of Scuba Professional is that, if you get the safety issues right, everything else, a solid income, a more fulfilling working life and a good reputation, will fall into place automatically.

As always, these are just the opinions of one man. You may not agree with everything I write but my main hope is that, even so, you may still find in these pages plenty of food for thought and debate.

Simon, July 2015

§1

Being Professional

1. Do You Have What It Takes?

B eing a scuba diving instructor is a wonderful line of work. You can genuinely change people's lives for the better. To be able to scuba dive and explore the world beneath the water is an incredible gift and if you are the one who places that gift in someone's hands, you earn their gratitude forever. Nobody ever forgets the name of the person who taught them to dive.

It is the sort of job that many people dream of but many pursue that dream without properly researching what they are letting themselves in for. Careful individuals who would normally look at every angle before applying for a job in their field of expertise will instead just drop everything and decide to become a scuba instructor on a whim. The advertising, after all, is irresistibly seductive, with sales pitches usually running along the following lines: -

"If you are a passionate scuba diver with a great, personable attitude looking to live an extraordinary life being in, around and under water – perhaps this is your calling. As an instructor with our training agency you will become one of the most sought after dive professionals in the world and, with the new divers you teach or assist, you will be able daily to relive the same excitement you had on your first dive. So, if you are burnt out from the constant stress of office life, why not trade it in for the opportunity of a diverse, rewarding career in scuba diving? And if you only want to teach scuba diving in the evenings and at weekends as part of an active and healthy lifestyle, while retaining your current job, then you can do that too."

What right-minded person could possibly say "no" to that? No wonder many do not even give it a second thought!

Vocation not Vacation

Notice that the emphasis in the sales pitch is placed squarely on the diving rather than the teaching. The advertisers also know what sells. "Passionate," "extraordinary,'" "excitement," "diverse," "rewarding," "active," "healthy;" these are all power words designed to capture the hearts and minds of folk doing jobs that offer few of these adjectives. The scuba diving industry is well aware that the vast majority of its recruits are people who have already had one or more previous careers; people who are on a quest for the elusive grail of "job satisfaction." If school teaching could advertise itself in this fashion, there would be many more folk signing up for a second career in education!

If you have never had the desire to teach, then you should think twice before becoming a dive instructor, because after you qualify and get a job as a dive instructor, teaching is what you will be spending most of your time doing. Yes, you will sometimes be underwater while you are teaching but you will not usually be doing dives that enthral you. Your office may be the ocean but it will mostly be the same patch of ocean day after day.

If you are not excited by the prospect of teaching, communicating the joy of this incredible sport to others and deriving immense satisfaction from seeing the look in their eyes when they conquer their fears and "get it," then you will not be a happy dive instructor. You will probably not stay a dive instructor for long and the considerable amount of time and money it took you to get there will have been wasted.

Ask yourself five questions.

1. Do you like people?

It is important that dive instructors really like people as their whole day is spent interacting with people. Many scuba instructors in the early days were not so much people who liked people; they were rather ex-military people who liked ordering other people around. If exercising power and control over others and bending them to your will is your thing then scuba diving in today's world will not suit you. Sympathy and empathy are the key words; if you can develop bonds easily and have the capacity to understand what someone is experiencing from within their frame of reference, you will make a good dive instructor.

2. Can you stay calm in any situation?

No matter what means you use to control or guide them, groups of divers are composed of free-thinking, unpredictable, excitable individuals who can disrupt your carefully laid plans in an instant. This is where your ability to stay calm will be tested. Your ability to be flexible (question 5) will also be put under serious examination as will your claim (question 1) that you really do like people.

3. Are you fair?

It is not your job to pick favourites among your students but to deal with each of them fairly and professionally. This takes us back again to question 1. You need to like all people; not just some of them!

4. Are you a confident communicator?

Whether it is mathematics, music or scuba diving, teachers in every field need to know their stuff and be confident in communicating their knowledge. Think about your teachers at school. Who were the ones from whom you learned most? What did they do to be so effective? Could you do the same?

5. Can you manage time?

The ability to use time efficiently is a crucial asset to a dive instructor. Whether you are teaching a course or leading a group of divers, you are always limited by time. You have to exercise time discipline yourself and ensure that your students and customers do likewise, all without spoiling the fun! It is a tough thing to do.

Here is an example of a typical three-dive day on a boat in the tropics. 8.00 leave dock: 9.00 arrive first site: 9.30 dive: 10.30 finish dive: 11.30 arrive second site: 12.00 dive: 1.00 finish dive and have lunch: 2.00 arrive third site: 2.30 dive: 3.30 finish dive: 4.30 return to dock

This is an 8.5-hour programme for 3 one-hour dives. The divers have paid for three full dives and, from a safety point of view, by 5.30 pm in the tropics the sun is too low for you to have any divers in the water. So you have very little room for error: even a slight delay in the schedule jeopardizes the whole day. When you work in diving, you learn to appreciate why time limits are set for fun dives and why sometimes the whip has to be cracked; (in the nicest way possible, of course!)

It Is You that Has to Decide

The dive centres and instructor trainers who run instructor courses do not talent spot. The fact that you have been accepted as a candidate does not mean that someone has seen that you have the right attitude, aptitude and personality to become a successful dive instructor. You have to decide this. The professionals' job is simply to bring as many people into the courses as possible and teach them how to pass the instructor exam. They are very good at this. Very few people fail.

So just because you have passed the exam and have a certificate and card saying that you are an instructor, this does not mean automatically that you are going to be successful or that you will enjoy it. There is quite a high dropout rate. Not all the hundreds of people who successfully complete a dive instructor course every year go on to have long-term careers in diving.

To be fair, not everyone who takes an instructor course is motivated by career change. Some people start their diver training and get carried along by the enthusiasm of the moment, the camaraderie of others and, it must be said, the salesmanship of the dive operation. Almost before they know it, they are taking the instructor exam. They may start by teaching a few friends and family but once a new generation of instructor candidates arrives in the dive centre they find themselves side-lined and often drift away from the sport, carrying with them some great memories and a line on their curriculum vitae.

Financially, it is really only worthwhile doing an instructor course if you genuinely intend to work in diving or teach people for real money on a full-time or part-time basis. You will not become a better diver just by doing an Instructor course, no matter which training agency you choose. The instructor course teaches you a training system, it will not improve your diving skills anywhere near as much as, for example, a cave diving course or a proper deep diving course.

Golden Gods and Goddesses

The impulse to become a scuba instructor may have come from observing professionals in action when you were a student or a customer. These golden gods and goddesses of the sea are impressive. They have the answers to all the questions, they see everything that goes on, are always around to offer help when you need it, and move around underwater effortlessly like long, sun-kissed fish. Nothing is ever a problem; life is full of fun and frolics.

This is of course an act. We play a role that our bosses and our clients expect us to play. Our job is to keep people safe, give them a good time and sell them the kind of relaxed, carefree lifestyle that Jimmy Buffett sings about. The images that accompany the sales pitch that I mentioned at the head of this chapter show gorgeous coral reefs (your office) and cool dudes and chicks in sunglasses (your colleagues) with the wind blowing in their hair as their speedboat carries them off to the next dive site (your meeting room.)

The images do not show what happens after the diving customers have returned to their hotels. This is when the real work begins: filling cylinders, washing and fixing equipment, doing the paperwork, nursing aches and pains and preparing for the next day. Believe it or not, it is work!

We do not tend to show customers everything that goes on in the background because that is not what they want or need to see. It spoils the myth that everyone is on vacation together. The perfect dive operation can be compared to a duck, serene and effortless on the surface, but with lots of unseen paddling going on beneath.

Home or Away?

For many folk, the main advantage in becoming a professional dive instructor is the opportunity to leave home and head for exotic tropical destinations to work in resorts or on boats. Bear in mind though that urban dive centres also need staff and can offer both permanent or part-time opportunities for instructors. However, while staff turnover in tropical dive resorts can be very fast and vacancies arise constantly as instructors move on or burn out, the same cannot be said for most urban dive centres, where staff members are likely to be far more long term.

So, if you are thinking of working for an urban dive centre, make sure you have a guaranteed place before you take your instructor course. Bear in mind also that being a full time employee of an urban dive store means minding the store, selling equipment, handing out rental gear, filling cylinders and carrying out maintenance, as well as teaching classes and running trips. So picking up qualifications in areas other than teaching will make you eminently more employable.

If your idea is to keep your regular job and teach classes to earn extra money, then again do some research first. Urban dive centres will usually already have at least one instructor on staff as well as a cadre of part-time instructors that they have been working with for a long time. If anyone contacts the store wanting to learn to dive, the dive centre will pass the student along to these instructors. They will not be interested in you as a new part-time instructor unless you have your own source of students and thus new customers for the dive centre. They are a business, after all. Of course, later, when you have paid your dues and become established, the dive centre may pass students on to you. But consider this as a bonus. It should not be part of your business plan. Therefore, ideally you should make sure you have good, hitherto-untapped sources of potential scuba diving students before you invest in your instructor course.

Pay & Conditions

You may have noticed also that the typical sales pitch for scuba instructors does not mention money. Salaries and benefits vary widely but, generally speaking, diving jobs are not well paid and this is another reason why you really need to have a vocation for teaching in order to survive in this line of work. You need to have the same sort of dedication that other professionals like nurses or schoolteachers have, in order to endure very long, difficult working hours for little financial reward.

In the early days, you may have to take what you are offered but, as in any field of work, make sure before you sign up for a job that you know what the conditions are. Then decide if they are acceptable and do you best to ensure that your bosses keep to their word. Get as much as you can in writing with a signature. Of course, you have to be professional and keep to your side of the deal too.

Be wary of accepting positions that give you no days off or wages that are ridiculously low. There are some cynical dive operators out there all too willing to take advantage of the wide-eyed enthusiasm of newly fledged instructors. If you work every waking minute for next to nothing then you will probably burn out very quickly. The cynical operators do not care: every week the system churns out new instructors to replace you.

There is another consideration. If you do not have enough respect for yourself to ensure that your rewards in monetary terms as well as lifestyle terms are commensurate with your efforts, it is unrealistic to expect others to treat you with respect. Dive instructor colleagues will not thank you for helping to bring down still further a salary bar that is already much too low.

As well as a salary, an urban dive centre will often offer commission on sales and student fees for teaching classes. They may also provide you with your own equipment while you are working for them so that you act as a kind of runway model for the brands they sell.

Instructors working in resorts and on boats will often have accommodation and meals included in their benefits package. Salaries may be low but they can be supplemented by guest tips. Many operators will boast that their instructors are so good that they earn as much in tips as they do in salary. This, of course, can be a reflection of the low salary rather than the high tips. Be aware, also, that not all nations have a tipping culture so the amount you earn in gratuities will depend on where your customers come from.

A key pay-related issue that you should clarify when you apply for a job in another country is the question of who will be paying for your work permit. In many cases, the work permit does not actually belong to the employee but to the company. That is, it permits the company to employ you but it does not permit you to leave the company and work for someone else in the same country. This is a tricky situation that involves some mutual trust. If you pay for the permit and you get fired before your contract is completed, you lose your money. If the company pays for it and you quit early, the company loses.

Doing It For the Diving

If you want to become a scuba instructor just in order to do some great diving, then as soon as you qualify you can join the back of the line of folk queuing up for the few jobs around where this is possible. You would be much better off studying and working hard to get a great job in a completely different line of work. The sort of job that will give you the financial resources to go off on dive holidays all the time and actually pay dive instructors to do the hard work and take you around.

Even when you find a dream diving job, it rarely lives up to expectations. Mark, a top underwater photographer and instructor, once got a job that earned him several hundred dollars a day running the dive operations on a super yacht. However, on day one he found out that his own accommodation on this five star boat was substantially less than five star. He was given a hammock behind a sheet in the owner's wife's gym, above a bank of fridge freezers.

The Divemaster Myth

Part of the mythology that the scuba diving world touts to outsiders says that, if you do not want to teach or work with brand new divers, then you can just become a divemaster, looking after experienced divers and showing them around. It is actually very difficult to find a PAID job in scuba diving if you only have divemaster qualifications. Generally speaking, the only people who work for money as guides without instructor qualifications are people from poorer countries who work for extremely low salaries and cannot afford instructor training course fees which, wherever the courses are run, are set at first-world levels.

Health Issues

As a scuba instructor you will dive between fifteen and thirty times a week, racking up huge amounts of water time and developing a high level of dive fitness. There are risks involved in doing this and instructors will of course mitigate these wherever possible, for instance, by ensuring the key elements of their equipment are in perfect shape and keeping well rested and hydrated before and after each dive. But, it is a fact that professionals are more frequent visitors to the recompression chambers than their amateur counterparts. Many long-term dive instructors have chronic aches and pains accumulated over years of submitting their bodies to constant pressure changes.

Sometimes, as an instructor, your duties require you to do things that you would certainly not advise other divers to do. For instance, you will tell your beginner students about the inherent risk in diving a yo-yo profile with frequent ascents and descents and then on dive four of their course you will escort all six of them individually as they practice emergency out-of-air ascents to the surface from 6m (20ft), going up and down several times, (yes, like a yo-yo,) in that part of the water column where the pressure change, and therefore the risk, is greatest.

Similarly, no diving manual would ever condone the practice of doing a deep bounce dive incorporating substantial physical stress followed a few minutes later by a longer dive to the same depth but this is something that instructors in some places do several times a day, as they set the shot line into a wreck and then ascend in order to pick up the group and descend again to guide them around the site.

The Positives

Why do I seem to accentuate the negative aspects of becoming a scuba instructor over the positives? I do this in an attempt to balance out the rosy picture that the scuba diving industry paints to draw people into its net.

Thousands of people happily earn a living in scuba diving, getting kick after kick passing on the joys of this sport to new divers or showing people the amazing things that live beneath the surface of our lakes, seas and oceans. Most of the people you meet as a dive professional are outgoing, adventurous and fun loving. Dive boats and dive centres are fantastic places to work.

As I will describe later in the chapter "The Road from Scuba Instructor to Dive Professional," to get on in the scuba diving world, you will need to learn your trade and never stop learning. You will need to market yourself and create your own networks just as you would in any other walk of life. But what you will need more than anything else is to really want to do this thing! You will need to have the vocation to keep you smiling and energised through the difficult days, finding solace in the fact that you are doing a job you love. Because, without that vocation, you really would be better off looking for another line of work.

Be professional by

Doing a lot of research before planning a new career as a scuba instructor.
Recognising that the job primarily involves teaching.
Asking yourself if you have a teaching vocation.

2. Which Instructor Training Agency?

Although scuba diving as we know it was invented by two French men, the first scuba diving club was established in the United Kingdom and the first people to create a network of people whose primary job was to teach diving for money were Americans. Today, however, the vast majority of people who learn to dive are not native French or English speakers. Scuba diving has truly gone global.

There are a whole host of diver training and certification agencies; well over 150 worldwide. Some are huge, multi-national corporations that cover the globe; others are much smaller and represent the vision of just a small group of people. Some agencies are state-affiliated but most are privately owned and operated. Some only operate in one country and one language and are unknown elsewhere.

The one thing they all have in common, however, is that they are businesses, commercial operations that need to recruit and train a sales force to sell their products so that they can make sales and earn money. In scuba diving, the instructors and dive centre owners who are affiliated with an agency are its sales force.

Curiously, despite the substantial number of options available, most prospective scuba instructors never go through any sort of research and selection process to choose the company with whom they will tie their future careers. They just go for the agency that they did their diver training with, as if there were no alternatives.

We Want YOU!

In fact, as a prospective instructor looking for an agency to train and teach with, you are a buyer in a buyers' market. All the agencies want YOU! An agency succeeds on the quality and quantity of its instructors and instructor trainers and it needs to sell itself to you. There is no selection process that you have to pass. As long as you have the requisite diving experience, every agency will leap at the chance to include you in one of its instructor development programmes.

So you are in the enviable position of being able to shop around but what are you looking for? Here are a few ideas. Compare what each agency does to make it easier for an instructor to sell its courses. How much advertising does it do? What is its reputation within the dive industry and outside? Find out if it is even known outside the diving industry, as this might have a huge impact on your ability to attract non-divers to the sport. What are the training materials like? Would they impress your customers? How much does it cost you to teach a course through the agency; what are the certification fees; how much do the course materials cost; what annual dues do you have to pay to retain your membership?

All scuba diving training agencies essentially sell the same product, yet they all define themselves as unique. Find out how each agency positions itself in the market. What is its unique selling point (USP); does its USP matter to you: would it have any real influence on a diver trying to choose between you and an instructor representing a different training agency?

On a more sober note, you might also want to find out what support a training agency will give you if an accident takes place while you are teaching a course. You can also ask what procedures the agency has in place to maintain quality control among its affiliated instructors and dive centres. After all, if a fellow instructor acts in a way that damages the reputation of a training agency then this can have an impact on you too as a representative of that agency.

Future Proofing

Assuming you are thinking in terms of a long term career in scuba diving, before you decide you may wish to consider the extent to which each training agency is future proofing its business by embracing online learning and adapting its ways to suit changing customer preferences. Technology-driven change has swept over many industries and scuba diving is not immune. More and more divers now prefer to study diving theory on the Internet instead of in a classroom and this is highly likely to become the norm in the near future, with attending a traditional classroom session becoming as rare as, say, renting a movie from a local video store.

Training agencies and instructors are wrestling with how to assimilate this development and this is not an easy process. Most are used to operating systems and pricing structures that have served the industry well over the last fifty years. But there is little doubt that diver training is on the cusp of change.

Educational institutions in other fields have benefitted enormously from the online learning revolution It has given them access to student bodies far greater than those they traditionally spoke to. For example, the University of California launched an online course in Behavioural Psychology in 2014 and within days had recruited over 100, 000 students all over the world to take the course. The students benefit too by having access via various media to vast resources of knowledge. They also have the freedom to explore these resources without restrictions of time or location.

Some diver training agencies see the positives and are adjusting their procedures accordingly. Others focus instead on the negative aspects of the new technology and are therefore more cautious. Among other things they fear the adverse commercial consequences of reduced physical student interaction with dive centres and instructors and worry about losing control over their training materials.

My advice would be to research the options, ask around and pick an agency whose views on online education most closely reflect your own.

Does Size Matter?

A significant strength of small and medium enterprises in any field is their ability to adapt quickly to new ideas and new technologies and this is certainly the case in scuba diving. Even as a new instructor with a smaller training agency you may know the owners personally and be able to influence how the agency does things or even contribute to its training materials.

On the other hand, as a relatively junior member of one of the large multi-national agencies, it is unlikely that any ideas you may have will have an impact on agency policy or practice. It may be very hard even to get your voice heard by the decision makers, protected as they are by levels of bureaucracy, like the leaders of any large company.

Progression through the ranks is slow too in the larger agencies, as there are many people waiting in line ahead of you and they are all keen to protect their position in the company structure. For large companies in general, maintaining the hierarchy is an important factor in ensuring stability.

Here is an excellent example: a few years ago one major training agency adopted a new range of programmes. The agency had very few top trainers with experience of this type of diving on its books but it had a larger number of more junior trainers with a lot of relevant experience. There was much internal debate. If the agency fast-tracked the more junior trainers to the top of the tree, there was a better chance that the new programmes would succeed immediately. But, there was the danger that this would cause discontent among the agency's more senior members.

In the end, the agency chose not to disrupt the existing hierarchy and, instead, they gave their top trainers a short introductory course and threw them in at the deep end, so to speak. Consequently, the new programmes took a long time to take off properly. Most large bureaucracies in any field of human activity would make a similar decision.

Early Opportunities

Some agencies are new and can offer opportunities for faster progress through the ranks. If you join an agency in its early days then your seniority will derive from the time you have spent with the agency rather than your overall teaching experience.

If you teach in a part of the world where one of the smaller training agencies has no presence, you may even be able to buy a local franchise for the agency. At the DEMA show in Las Vegas recently, an instructor trainer friend from Singapore was offered the franchise for a European diver-training agency that had decided to branch out into Asia. All he did to earn this invitation was stop by the agency's stand as he walked the show. Opportunities abound; you just need to be in the right place at the right time.

Not all agencies operate according to the same business model. Some have a centralised, top-down structure where it is the "World Headquarters" that directs policy, produces training materials, approves marketing initiatives and controls everything. Other agencies give satellite franchises much more autonomy and there are some whose materials vary so greatly in appearance from country to country that only the logo tells you which agency they pertain to. You may be able to contribute much more to the direction of a decentralised agency.

All these considerations, of course, only apply if you are thinking of building a career in scuba diving. What if your ambitions are less long-term?

Forget the Career: I Just Want to Work in Paradise for a While

Like many people, you may decide to become a dive instructor just so that you can take a break away from your usual life and go off to live and work in some exotic destination that you have always dreamed about.

If so, then you need to conduct your training agency research more locally. Find out which are the best-represented agencies in the country or region you want to live in. These are the agencies you should focus on. The more centres your chosen agency has in the area, the more likely it is that you will find work.

Local conditions often dictate which agencies dive centres choose to affiliate with. For instance, there is an island with over 300 dive centres where one agency has an enormous presence simply because the regional headquarters is located on that island.

Individuals can have an impact too. With the more decentralised agencies, someone charismatic, pro-active and with a service-orientated background can take a regional franchise, recruit a large network of dive centres and instructors and generate a level of success out of proportion to the agency's status worldwide. Of course, if that person should move on, the comparative weakness of the agency internationally might leave the local network poorly serviced.

I Have No Idea Where I Want to Go

If you have no idea where you want to work as a dive instructor and if, at this early stage, you want to get some experience before you start thinking about career goals, the agency that will give you the best chance of getting a job anywhere in the world is PADI.

PADI is the largest training agency; the one that has most affiliated dive centres and resorts and the one that first introduced the concept that diving was not just for an athletic elite. PADI was the first commercially orientated agency and it is one of very few dive industry entities that actively market to non-divers in non-scuba-related media. Because of this, many non-divers think that there is actually only one training agency. "I'm going to do my PADI," they say.

Instructor Crossovers

Once you are an instructor with one agency, there is nothing to stop you from joining another, apart from the expenses involved in "crossing over" and having to pay multiple agency membership fees each year. You can become a better instructor by learning a different system and new techniques and having multiple affiliations will make you more employable. However, again, do a little research first. Many training agencies are almost carbon copies of each other and are distinguished by not much more than different logos and colour schemes. At the instructor level, none of the agencies will have any objection to you holding multiple instructor certifications, although you should not expect anyone from your original agency to actively suggest this.

It is almost certain that if you apply for a new job with a dive operator that runs courses through a training agency that you are not affiliated with, you will be asked to do a crossover. As this can be an expensive process, before you agree, match the costs against your monthly wage to see if it is worth your while. You could ask if your new employers will pay for the crossover but they may be reluctant, perhaps because they have done this in the past and the instructor then resigned soon afterwards. It might, however, be possible to reach a compromise whereby you pay for the crossover in the first instance and then they reimburse you a portion of the expenses with your salary each month.

When you cross over, some agencies require you do another full instructor course, usually repeating much of what you have already done. Others give you some credit for previous experience but still ask you to do at least part of their course. One agency encourages experienced instructors recruited to its ranks to undergo cave diver training to improve their skills. It works!

Finally, a word of caution: some training agencies offer paid paper crossovers whereby they certify you as one of their instructors or instructor trainers without requiring you to show off your knowledge or demonstrate your skills and teaching ability. All you have to do is hand over the money and sign your name to a form.

Be very wary of any agency that takes this approach. You have to question the motivation. The pitch is often delivered in such a way as to make you feel that you have been "head-hunted." It can be tempting as it plays to your ego. After all, we all have one. But ask yourself, are you honestly someone whose experience, reputation and following make you such an asset that the agency will do anything to have you on board? If this is not the case then why are they doing this? Are they making similar offers to almost anybody? If so, then at least some of your fellow recruits are likely to be those who have been rejected by or expelled from other training agencies and are looking for a new banner to teach under where standards are lower and fewer questions are asked. The agency will soon become known as a last resort for the disaffected and both its quality and its reputation will plummet. You do not want to have any part in this.

Be professional by

Recognising that as an instructor you are a valuable commodity.
Knowing that you have choices.

3. The Road from Instructor to Scuba Professional

I'm a scuba instructor! I've done it! I have reached the summit of my profession! I have worked hard, acquired some impressive skills and gained a lot of knowledge. I have also spent quite a lot of money on courses, equipment and exam fees. But now I am done with the training. I have achieved what I wanted to achieve and at last it's time to reap the rewards of all my efforts. People are going to line up around the block to take courses from me."

Such optimistic sentiments are common in new instructors, especially as so many people these days go from new diver to new instructor very quickly, often in a matter of months, and they have been carried along to their goal by a tide of encouragement, momentum and adrenalin.

However, for many instructors, almost before the ink is dry on the examiner's signature, reality sets in. Throughout their training everyone has been making them feel very special but now that feeling fades away and is replaced by the dawning realisation that they are but one of a multitude of fledgling scuba instructors released into the world that month and that, out there, ahead of them in the pecking order are the countless multitudes of scuba instructors that preceded them.

In fact, that is not actually the case. Most of those multitudes that passed this way before them are no longer working in diving. As I mentioned in the first chapter, "Do You Have What It Takes?" many new instructors quickly drop out. The drive and enthusiasm that carried them to their instructor card disappear or are redirected elsewhere. They may teach one or two courses to the friends, neighbours or workmates who have been badgering them to teach them on the cheap once they get qualified, but when their first annual renewal comes around, they will let it slide and, in years to come, they will only use their instructor status for bragging rights or to try to scam a discount from a dive centre.

It's a Long Road

Why do they lose motivation? Let's assume for the sake of argument that they had some genuine motivation in the first place and that they were not just in it to get a card and a certificate to hang on the glory wall. Often they lose their way because, misguidedly, they assume that completion of the instructor course and success in the exam represent the end of the road. But in fact, to paraphrase Winston Churchill, this is not the end, it is not even the beginning of the end; it is only the end of the beginning!

After the instructor exam, there is still a long way to go before instructors reach the level of comfort required to deal easily with a group of student divers. Up to that point, teaching an open water diving course is tough; it demands a great deal of preparation, attention to detail and concentration, especially when you have problem students. Perhaps this is where some people lose their enthusiasm, when they find out that it is so much harder than they expected and decide that they are therefore not cut out for the job. Others, perhaps, find belatedly that they do not have the necessary levels of patience or altruism to be a teacher. Of course, they should have identified this before investing in the training but it is hard for potential scuba professionals to find objective guidance. The training agencies' promotional material understandably glosses over anything that might cause people to think twice about signing up.

Being New

Neophyte scuba divers have no way of distinguishing between an instructor who passed his exam last week and one who has been plying his trade for many years. They automatically assume that every dive instructor is an underwater God or Goddess, a Neptune or Aphrodite reborn, half-(wo)man-half-fish.

Even if you are a brand new instructor, your students will accord you this status and confer upon you wisdom that you are all too aware you do not possess. It is very important that you don't start believing the propaganda yourself or, worse, pressure yourself into thinking that you somehow have to live up to their billing!

In the early days you may feel that you are expected to know everything. The divers you are guiding and the students you are teaching bombard you with questions, and not always about diving. You are expected to be omniscient! A guide who used to work in the Red Sea once told me that often, when she was up on deck leaning on the rail and watching a super tanker or a big container ship cruise by, one of the guests would invariably join her and, after a few moments silence, would ask her where the ship was going or what it was carrying on board!

No-one can know everything of course. The problem when you begin a new job or an old job in a new location is that you are not sure what you are supposed to know and what you cannot reasonably be expected to know. The lack of confidence engendered by this uncertainty often leads you to try and bluff your way through. This in turn makes you anxious that you might be found out to be a fraud.

The answer to this dilemma is not to worry about saying "I don't know," even if that might cause a crack to appear in the super-human, all-knowing shell that your customers have built around you. Then find out the answer to the question, so that next time it is asked you will know what to say. People are mostly the same; the things they ask are mostly the same. It won't be long before your omniscience is genuine.

As a guide, it is very common to be tasked by your dive centre to take divers to a site you have never visited before. Of course, this should never happen and dive operations should have training systems in place for new staff to familiarise them with the sites before they have to guide divers around them, but this rarely happens. The pressure of business usually means that most instructors are put to work alone as soon as they get off the plane and expected to learn as they go along. When this happens to you, try first to persuade an off-duty colleague to come along with you to help. If you cannot find someone, get as much information as you can in advance from more experienced colleagues and do your best.

Build a Career

As in any profession, you need to build a career from the bottom up. As a new instructor you are far from the finished product and it is essential that you keep making progress. Keep learning. You were not taught everything there is to know about diving in your instructor course and in the courses you took leading up to that. Don't just parrot what you read in your manuals. Make sure you understand the background to what you teach. Read widely, especially books about the psychology and physiology of diving. Understand decompression theory. Be open to new ideas and ways to do things but don't just believe every new theory you come across. Question everything.

You need to focus on improving your personal diving skills so that they become instinctive and so that you can devote 100% of your attention to your students. At the same time you need to develop your underwater management and control skills. Learn to observe and interpret behaviour so you can anticipate problems before they occur. These two goals are connected. If you have excellent personal diving skills then it is easier to acquire excellent dive management skills. It is amazing how much more you see and how much more time you have to deal with problems once you have achieved mastery of your own buoyancy, movement and positioning in the water. I return to this in more detail later in the chapter.

You also need to learn to become a real teacher, learning on the job. This is tough because you will usually receive little guidance from your peers or bosses. Opportunities to work with and learn from more experienced colleagues are rare in scuba diving as most instructors work alone. If you ever get a chance to do this, seize it!

A career building tip: if you do not already have a commercial background, then do some small business courses so you understand at least the basics of accountancy, marketing, staff management and maintaining cash flow. This knowledge is essential if you are planning to work independently. It will also make you much more marketable as an employee. Dive centres and resorts are primarily businesses after all. You will have to look outside diving for these courses, as unfortunately there is very little such training available within the scuba diving industry itself. There should be.

How To Get a Job

Ratchet your expectations down to the minimum in terms of salary and benefits. Dive operations realised long ago that people will actually pay them to do the sort of work you are hoping to get paid for. So, unless you have other very marketable skills, you may not initially be treated with the sort of respect and admiration that the folk who ran your instructor training promised you.

Use connections; talk to the people who trained you, contact the dive operations you have visited. Look at the life skills you may have acquired elsewhere over the years that may have nothing to do with diving itself but which dive operations desperately need. I once took on a guy who came to me looking for a job as a divemaster. I put him on an excellent salary, gave him an apartment to live in and financed his instructor training. Why? I did this because he was a former aircraft mechanic. With him on staff, not only did I have a new member of the teaching and guiding staff, I had a qualified engineer who could take care of the maintenance of all the dive gear, the compressor, the gas mixing station, the shop vehicles and the boat engines. He was worth every penny he earned and more.

Owners and operators of dive liveaboards frequently bemoan the fact that most of the people who apply for dive guide or cruise director vacancies do not have the sort of qualifications they are looking for. Neither of these positions involves much actual teaching so instructor qualifications are not the priority. Far more important for the guide position are an encyclopaedic knowledge of the marine life in the region where the liveaboard operates and the ability to seek out the sort of animals that divers want to see and photograph. The best guides have, as we say in the trade, "good eyes!"

For cruise director positions, operators are looking for instructors with people skills but a hospitality industry or, better still, a hotel management background would catapult you to the top of the list of candidates. If this background included work on cruise ships, then you would definitely find yourself in demand.

If you have good language skills, you will find that you can negotiate higher pay and better benefits. Again, take the time to do some research. Study where divers who speak the languages you have in your arsenal tend to travel and look especially for destinations which they are just discovering. That is where you will find dive operations looking for people who can help them cater to this new market. Dive magazines are a good place to start. Look for articles on "new" destinations or "best-kept secrets." These are often established places that this particular language market is just discovering.

For example, a few years ago Russian divers discovered the wonders of my home island Bali and local dive centres were all looking for Russian speakers to help them sell to this new group of travellers. Today, as I write, the emerging market is for Chinese divers and operators are all looking to take on Mandarin speaking staff.

Couple Up?

Something that many dive professionals do is team up and job search as a double act. Most double acts are a male / female duo who are also romantically involved but you will also encounter all male or all female couples, whether romantically involved or not, who sell themselves as an instructional or management team.

By pooling their skills and resources they expand on their individual skill sets. For operators, there are both advantages and disadvantages to employing a couple. They save money because, generally speaking, these two workers take up the same accommodation space as one. As long as they get on well together, the operator does not have to worry about managing employee relationships, at least as far as these two are concerned. However, if the couple's friendship breaks down then this can spill over and create problems within the team as a whole. Operators have to bear in mind too, that if one of the couple becomes unhappy with their job, then the chances are that they will lose two staff instead of one.

Build Your CV

Enhance your qualifications. Some training agencies have procedures in place whereby instructors can self-certify themselves as specialty instructors simply by sending in a log of a couple of dozen relevant dives and paying a processing fee.

You should take advantage of administrative procedures like this to enhance your resume. You are not being dishonest unless you fake your dive logs and most agencies provide excellent instructor guides for you to work from. But do not expect anyone to be impressed by your status as a navigation or night diving specialist. In fact, it is best to pick and choose rather than spend money on having a list of qualifications as long as your arm, many of which you will never need. It is a constant source of frustration to training agencies that divers do not do more specialty courses. They blame dive shops and instructors for failing to market them adequately but possibly the low take-up rate is due rather to divers not perceiving much value in some of them.

The NITROX diver course is a big seller on liveaboards and in holiday destinations so make sure you have that specialty under your belt but apart from that, it is a question once again of doing some research. If you are applying for jobs in a destination where there are plenty of shipwrecks then get some wreck diving experience and apply for a wreck instructor ticket. If you are interested in places that offer a lot of wall diving, then you might expect requests for deep diver courses.

To improve your skills, however, practice, practice, practice! Dive as much as you can, in as many different environments and conditions as you can. Stay within your personal comfort zone but try to push the envelope little by little. Once you have achieved mastery of your skills in the open ocean within the 40m (132ft) depth range with no decompression limits, then look to challenge yourself further and go on to the next level, technical diving.

Even as an experienced scuba instructor, you will feel like a complete beginner again when you embark on technical diving. Prepare yourself for this feeling and enjoy it! Don't let your ego get in the way. I remember a few years ago putting one of Asia's most accomplished and experienced instructor trainers, a man with over 4,000 logged dives, through a TRIMIX course and watching him panic and surface twice during the pool sessions. To the man's eternal credit, he gathered himself, swallowed his pride and persevered, eventually becoming a world-renowned technical instructor.

If you did not think your skills could improve any further, you will surprise yourself. When you return to single cylinder no-stop diving after having acquired the ability to manage multiple gases in multiple cylinders within the virtual overhead environment imposed by a decompression ceiling, you will truly appreciate how much you have learned and how far you have come.

You will also have acquired further knowledge that you can pass on to divers in your charge. There are plenty of things that technical divers learn that all divers would find useful, such as how to calculate their breathing rate and air consumption, different ways of setting up and streamlining their equipment or alternative ways of finning to reduce environmental disturbance.

Climb the Training Ladder

At the same time as you are improving your personal skills, you can be developing your teaching and people-management skills not only by instructing divers but also by passing on what you have learned to the next generation of scuba instructors. Talk to a local Course Director / Instructor Trainer (CD/IT) about assisting him or her when they next run an instructor course and step onto the first rung of the ladder towards becoming a CD/IT yourself. They will welcome your input. It is highly beneficial for instructor candidates to be able to receive advice from someone who has recently experienced what they are about to go through. You will be learning too, both from the candidates themselves as they ask questions and make mistakes and also from the CD/IT as you listen again to the lectures. It is a good idea to seek out a different CD/IT from the one who managed your own instructor course, as you are likely to pick up new teaching techniques and people-management methods.

In all training agencies the path to CD/IT is well laid out and involves acquiring a mix of diving and teaching experience. There are usually several levels of progression and it is a good idea to start developing your own profile and reputation within your chosen agency and establish a network of contacts, as you are likely to encounter an element of politics as you progress. CD/ITs are usually appointed on the basis of geographical need. Training organisations always try to ensure that there are sufficient CD/ITs in an area to meet demand but not so many that they find themselves competing for business. It is a difficult balance and you need to be sufficiently well connected to be able to identify areas of need and position yourself accordingly.

Develop the Ultimate Skills

In the meantime, even as you approach the heights as a professional beware of neglecting your personal development. The ultimate skill level in recreational scuba diving is overhead environment diving, which requires exceptional comfort and control in the water. Many divers love to explore inside shipwrecks and cave diving is at the same time the most demanding and most rewarding of all disciplines. Divers frequently ask me if they should do a wreck diver course or a cave diver course in order to obtain the skills to dive in an overhead environment and my answer is usually, "both!"

You do a wreck diving course to learn about shipwrecks and you do a cave diver course to dive in cave systems and develop superb skills. The best place in the world to do cave diver training is Central Florida, in the area around Lake City. Why? Because the instructors in that area were responsible for developing many of the techniques and much of the equipment that all scuba divers use today, such as octopus regulators and BCDs. Also, the cave systems here are deep enough and extensive enough to give you the kind of lengthy swim time and decompression time you need to complete during a good cave course.

I would add another caveat here, in case you are attracted by the idea of eventually specialising in teaching at the high end of the spectrum, such as deep rebreather diving, wreck penetration or cave diving. It takes considerable investment to get to the point where you can teach at these levels, the courses are often very long and you will rarely have more than one or two students at a time. However, you are restricted in the amount you can charge for your courses as you are often competing for students with professionals who also have other income streams or highly qualified amateur instructors who have highly paid full-time jobs. It is difficult to survive only on high-end courses. Those who do succeed because of their reputation, established over a long time.

Save, Save, Save!

Money is an important factor in enabling you to enjoy a full career in scuba diving. Many instructors who drop out of diving do so because they have not taken their finances seriously and are forced to leave the work and the life they love and return to the non-diving world simply on economic grounds. As I said before, scuba diving jobs are not well paid. Look at what the contributors to the "Alternatives to Instruction" chapter have to say on the subject. But that does not mean that you need to struggle. Many dive jobs take you to remote places where there are few entertainment options and, although your wages may be small, your board and lodging will be provided free of charge so you will have no expenses. There is a good chance too that your wages will be supplemented by tips. You therefore have a great opportunity to save money. You might want to build up an investment portfolio, buy a small apartment back home to rent out or even save up to one day start your own dive business and become an employer rather than an employee. I know of one instructor who by her late twenties had managed to save up a nest egg of 30,000 euros in five years.

However, for every instructor I have met who has managed to save money, I have met nine who do not have a penny to their names after a decade or more working in the sport. This is what I call the "oil-field" syndrome, as it is a pattern of behaviour that I first noticed when I was working in the Arabian Gulf many years ago.

Even if you are diving every day among glorious reefs and wake up every morning to the sort of view that most people only ever see on a screen saver, working in a remote location that offers little variety in the daily routine can become boring. So you start to dream of the things you will do on your time off, the expensive toys you will buy and the dive destinations you want to visit without pesky customers to look after.

The guests that you interact with on a daily basis do not help. In fact, they are largely, albeit unwittingly, responsible for creating some of the desires that may impoverish you and render it impossible for you to escape from the "paradise trap" that you are in. They will speak of places they have dived that will inspire your dreams of exotic travel; they will turn up with camera systems that create fabulous images and video that you want to imitate; and they will arrive with expensive dive equipment, titanium regulators, state-of-the-art dive computers, even rebreather systems, that you will envy.

It is a fact of life that in the world of scuba diving, the amateurs are vastly better off financially than the professionals. However, they envy the life-style of the professionals, while the professionals envy the amateurs' wealth. Sitting at the back of my dive shop in Guam, enjoying happy hour at the end of a wonderful diving day, one of my customers, a lawyer from Hong Kong, an investment banker from New York or a realtor from San Francisco perhaps, would say something along the lines of, "you are so lucky; you have it all. I wish I could have your life." And I would answer, in jest of course, "you can have it. I'll swap you one year of my life here for your salary for one year. Then I'll retire!"

Diving Needs You!

The dive industry needs professionals, people like you who have chosen to buy this book, people who see being a dive instructor as a career which, like any other profession, you need to work at to become truly proficient. It is exciting; it is a career that many envy and a life that can bring you rewards beyond the reach of most people. But it takes a great deal of focus and determination to succeed.

Be professional by

Being prepared to work to build your career in scuba diving as you would in any other walk of life.
Always being ready and willing to learn and make progress.
Being careful with your personal finances.

4. Career Survival: 7 Tips for Staying in the Game

An oft-quoted maxim holds that "there are old divers and there are bold divers: but there are no old, bold divers." This is a sweeping generalisation of course but, like many maxims, it holds a kernel of truth. History suggests that to survive a long career in scuba diving, there are a few things you need to do.

I talk a lot about technical diving in this chapter, primarily because in any calendar year the majority of those listed in the roll call of fatalities among serious and professional divers will be people who died doing dives that are beyond the scope of standard sport diving.

I illustrate some points with true stories of real divers, some of whom are no longer around. My aim in quoting their example is not to criticise but to show how we can learn from the mistakes they made and the traps they fell into and make sure that we avoid following in their footsteps.

Tip 1: Don't Take Shortcuts

Familiarity breeds contempt, or so the old cliché goes. Complacency is often the counterbalance to experience and this is one reason why diving accidents befall just as many experts as beginners.

Some might argue that statistically the more you do something; the greater is the chance that something will go wrong. Those who make such claims do not understand the concept of safe scuba diving. The way we dive and the way we teach diving is based completely on analysing everything that could possibly go wrong and making sure that a diver has the skills, the mental strength, the physical capacity and the equipment to deal with it. If you dive the right way with the right gas, the right equipment and the right state of mind each time the odds do not change no matter how much you dive. The problem is that we are human and one of the primary drivers that generate progress in our species is the desire to find an easier way to do things. So we are constantly tempted to take shortcuts.

Fear is also a key human driver and when we start diving, fear acts as a key motivator making us careful and keeping us safe. But the more dives we make without incident, the less we fear and the more we become convinced that we may be somehow immune, special or indestructible. That is when we start looking for easier options. We start asking ourselves questions like: "Do I really need to bring that back up light I have never used?" or "This rebreather has never failed me – why do I keep burdening myself with an open circuit bailout that I have never deployed?" or "I have been inside this wreck a hundred times; I don't need to bring a reel and line with me."

All experienced divers have reached a point where these thoughts have started to bubble up from the deepest reaches of their consciousness. It is only natural; these are the type of questions that have led to the development of Homo sapiens as a species. But, sadly, these are also the sort of thoughts that drive the type of behaviour that is celebrated every year in the Darwin Awards, so they have to be resisted.

Tip 2: Avoid "Back-Sliding"

Last year, I was invited to lunch by a couple of experienced technical instructors. They wanted my advice on an incident that had taken place the previous day on a wreck dive. One had sustained what seemed to be an oxygen-toxicity hit and the other instructor had rescued him, blowing off his final required decompression stops to bring him up after he had convulsed and lost his regulator at 6m (20ft). I asked for the details of the dive and they told me the wreck was on sand at 50m (165ft), they had been diving on air and they had been carrying decompression stage cylinders of NITROX 50 and pure oxygen (O2). They had done a little less than thirty minutes on the wreck and on ascent had switched to NITROX 50 at 20m (66ft) and O2 at 6m (20ft). The instructor had convulsed after only a couple of minutes at 6m (20ft.) Both survived the dive without any residual issues apart from a crisis of confidence, which is why they had called me. They were worried that someone could have an oxygen-toxicity hit after only a few minutes at a PO2 of 1.6.

I first asked if they were sure they were really at 6m (20ft) when the convulsion occurred and they assured me they were. In that case, I said, the most likely cause of the incident was that the instructor who had convulsed had made a mistake and switched to his O2 rather than his NITROX 50 at 20m (66ft). The diver said he was sure this wasn't the case and recounted a whole list of things he had done to make this impossible. However, when we all went back to the dive centre and checked the cylinders, it turned out that this was exactly what he had done.

In the early days of technical diving, breathing the wrong gas at the wrong depth was a common problem. Some survived; many didn't. Labelling and other conventions were established to reduce the chance of this happening but, we figured, human error being what it is, the best way to make sure you do not switch to the wrong decompression cylinder at depth is only to carry one, unless time and safety requirements absolutely insist that you carry more; for instance if your bottom gas is a hypoxic, helium rich mix.

For the dive these guys did, it was completely unnecessary for them to carry two decompression gasses. Either, the NITROX 50 or the O2 would have done the job just fine and having one gas would have had hardly any effect on the length of time required for their ascent. They were diving in calm, warm water: taking an extra few minutes to ascend was not going to compromise their safety.

I asked why they had chosen to use two decompression cylinders and the best answer I got was that it is more "tech" if you carry a stage on each side and they were making a video of the wreck so they wanted to look good. I suggested that a better solution would have been to carry two stages but put the same decompression gas in both.

I call this sort of thing "backsliding." It marks a return to practices and procedures that were previously rejected as being likely to lead to accidents: a step backwards in the evolutionary process.

More Backsliding

Here are other examples of common practices among dive professionals that I would classify as "backsliding."

When divers first started using multiple gases, it was not uncommon to encounter people who had decided that, instead of carrying their decompression gas in a side-slung independent cylinder, they would wear twin independent back mounted cylinders, one containing bottom gas and the other decompression gas. Many quickly found out to their cost that this was a really easy way of breathing the wrong gas at the wrong depth. It also, of course, meant that they had no bottom gas redundancy. I have no idea how anyone in diving today could still think that this is a good idea, yet the practice still crops up from time to time as each new generation gets bored of carrying stage cylinders and looks for a lazy way out, without thinking that maybe the lazy divers of previous generations have already passed this way and looking to find out what happened to them.

Another backsliding sin that many dive operations commit is not requiring that divers analyse and sign off on the content of their NITROX cylinders before a dive. When NITROX was first introduced to mainstream divers, this was a key element of the process. However, today it is becoming increasingly rare. This is probably due to a combination of things: the outstanding safety record of single cylinder NITROX diving and the need for operations to streamline their procedures as much as possible. It is true, if they are using a NITROX production system that cannot possibly produce a mix richer than NITROX 40 and the divers cannot go beyond 30m (100 ft), then, from an oxygen toxicity point of view, there is no risk for divers if their NITROX mix is not what they are told it is . However, if the operator is using pure O2 in a partial-pressure NITROX blending system and also makes decompression mixes for technical divers, then any cylinder that comes out of the compressor room could contain up to 100% pure O2.

Oxygen toxicity is not the only consideration. As divers commonly programme their dive computers to match the NITROX mix they are told they have in their cylinder, inaccurate mix information will mean that the decompression status information on the computer is completely irrelevant. To be blunt, the computer might not be in deco, but the diver might be! Actually, despite the fact that it is decorated with a NITROX band, the cylinder might actually not contain NITROX at all. It might just have boring 21% air in it. Failing to insist that divers check their own cylinders is not only unsafe, it represents a significant liability risk for dive operators that would seem to outweigh the advantage of having a more streamlined operation.

Tip 3: Resist Peer and Pupil Pressure

As professionals, we are subject to influences that can affect the way we dive, make us cut corners or do things we know are unsafe. Some of these influences are so subtle that we may not even notice them.

One of the levers that can change our attitudes insidiously is peer pressure. Rarely, this may be exerted directly, for instance when someone lays down a challenge. Mostly it is merely perceived. Someone talks about a dive they have done or becomes celebrated by achieving an envied goal. Perhaps a former student succeeds where you have not. A seed is sown, without you even being aware of it, which can develop into a force powerful enough to lead you to take unnecessary risks.

A few years ago, one of the pioneers of technical diving, a renowned instructor, caver, deep diver and influential author, fell in with a crowd who were into ultra deep air diving. In his books, the author had been a strong advocate of using TRIMIX for dives below 60m (200ft.) and had devoted whole chapters in his books to the perils of using air at extreme depths, especially now that TRIMIX was readily available. However, he felt a need to be accepted as a peer by the deep air folk and evidently decided that in order to gain their acceptance he had to be able to match the sort of achievements that they would all boast about over a beer or two when they got together after a diving day.

A gathering of the deep-air crew was to take place in the Red Sea and the author booked a place on a live-aboard in Egypt the week before and embarked on a programme of ultra deep air dives, each day's dive deeper than the last. Who knows what was going on in his head that week but there must have been some uncertainty. After all, he had been an ardent campaigner against the folly of deep air and now was practicing exactly the kind of diving that he had preached against. He must have had moments of doubt, particularly at depth when narcosis started to play its tricks on his mind. Anyway, one day he went in and never came back up again. He was last seen, far, far below the other divers in the group and heading downwards. No one knows what happened; his body was never found.

Pressure can also come from the divers you teach and I call this "pupil pressure." People are very willing to create heroes: they like to have someone to follow, someone to believe in. Once you have attained a certain status in the diving world, this someone may well be you. After all, it is relatively easy to build a legend in this small universe we operate in just by living long enough or being particularly adept at using social media. And that is fine; this is your career after all and a good image and a high profile will bring more work in.

Your students and those who follow you may think you are infallible and capable of incredible feats but, of course, their faith does not give you super-human powers. There is a real danger that, encouraged by their flattery, you can fall into the trap of believing your own propaganda but even if you resist the temptation, a more subtle danger still exists; that you might subconsciously perceive a need to live up to the image you have created and undertake dives that you are not really comfortable with.

Tip 4: Know When to Break the Chain

Every diving accident has a chain of events that lead up to it but often the chain is only visible afterwards. You do not always see a chain before an accident takes place, but if you do see one or if you only think you see one, you need to have the courage to break it, even if this might bring criticism from your students or others in your dive team.

Cave divers have a rule that seeks to eliminate the fear of recrimination and saves lives. This rule is that any diver can abort any dive at any time for any reason without having to explain themselves to anyone. When one of your team gives the turn signal, the rest of the team acknowledges and complies immediately, no questions asked, either at the time or subsequently. It does not matter if the threat to safety is genuine or not. For example, a diver may abort a dive simply as a result of misreading his contents gauge. The important thing is that if one member of the team believes there is a threat, then that belief in itself is enough to put the team at risk if it continues.

This is a principle that all instructors can apply to every dive, whether in an overhead environment or not.

Here is an example of an instance when I had to break the chain even before the divers got into the water.

A Dive Interrupted

The instructor in this story was with two students preparing for the final dive in their TRIMIX course when one of his divemasters arrived with the news that a diver that they all knew from another dive centre had died in the recompression chamber following an incident that had taken place the day before.

The students were nearby and overheard the conversation but said nothing. On the boat, they were quieter than usual and the instructor was concentrating on keeping everything normal, following the pattern of their earlier training dives, but the news of the diver's death was playing on his mind.

On arrival at the dive site, he saw that a strong current was running and that it had carried the site marker buoy underwater. The plan was that this buoy would be the ascent platform for the dive. The instructor noticed the students exchange a glance of concern.

He knew that the fact that they were undertaking a big dive would already be creating a certain level of anxiety, and that a strong current might lead to additional task-loading. He also guessed that the news of the diver's death might be a distracting factor for them, especially if they started to become stressed during the dive. Third, he was also concerned that the news might have an adverse impact on his own ability to concentrate.

He went over to where they were preparing and explained that he was cancelling the dive, citing all the reasons, including his doubts about his own state of mind. He was expecting them to be upset and object to this change in plan as they were due to fly out the following night and this cancellation would mean they couldn't complete the course on schedule. But instead, they responded with visible relief and thanked him profusely. They managed to change their flights and a couple of days later the final course dive was completed without a hitch. Who knows? Plan A might have turned out fine in the end but aborting the dive before any of them had even entered the water made it absolutely sure that what looked like a steadily cumulating series of stressors didn't end in disaster.

Tip 5: Keep Diving

As you become more senior in the scuba diving world and go into management or administration, you will find that you dive less than you used to. This means that your skills and instincts may not be as finely tuned as they once were.

This is particularly important to note if you like to do fairly serious dives. A number of accidents have befallen individuals who, although possessing world-class diving resumes, had not been actually diving that much before the dive that killed them.

One of these instances involved a very talented, serious, amateur diver who had a busy professional and family life and lived in a city where there was no diving available. So he would only dive on vacation and, because of his other responsibilities, this vacation time was necessarily short. Therefore he had to take advantage of every minute. He had no time to do practice or build up dives just for fun; all he had time for was to work on extending the range and degree of difficulty of his dives. His log in the last couple of years of his life made for astonishing reading with only a few dives a year but all to great depths and most in overhead environments until the most extreme dive he had ever made took his life.

No-one can say for sure if he would still have died on that dive if he had done more diving in the build up. However, it is a fact that when you do dive frequently you develop an early warning system, an intuition if you like, for problems affecting you and other divers around you that helps you identify potential emergencies and nip them in the bud. If you want to continue to do big dives after your career takes you behind a desk, then you need to make sure you take plenty of time out from your busy land life to keep your underwater instincts sharp.

Tip 6: Stay Fit

Like everyone, dive instructors get older and as we age our sport makes increasingly significant demands on our bodies. To become a diver in the first place, you need be mentally and physically fit so a necessary prescription for long-term survival in this sport is to stay fit, take care of your health, eat, drink and live sensibly, have annual check-ups that include a stress test and listen to your doctor. If the health check raises potential issues, cut back on the degree of difficulty and risk level of the dives you do.

There is another point worth making here. As professional scuba divers we are often used to depending on ourselves and making our own decisions, so we are often not good listeners and tend to resist advice that runs counter to our own opinions. You often hear people in the industry saying things like "it's my life! I can do what I like with it!"

However, it is not only you that suffers if you have a serious medical incident underwater. Your responsibility extends to those you dive with and those who try to rescue you. You also need to think of the dive industry as a whole as accidents often attract the attention of Government regulators who are always on the lookout for opportunities to interfere in what we do.

Tip 7: Know When to Step Back from the Edge

Finally, you need to know when to step back from the cutting edge. IANTD's Tom Mount is the best example I know of someone who did this. He was at the sharp end of cave exploration for many years and, during this time, experienced the loss of many of those who were there at the cutting edge with him. At one point, a variety of issues caused him to pull back and leave exploration to others. Of course he continued to dive and teach but he decided he was no longer willing to accept the level of risk that going where others have never been involves. He kept to that decision and this is certainly a key factor in his almost unparalleled longevity in the sport.

All of us are individuals and only you can know when it is the right time to cut down your risk exposure. But if you are aware of the fact that that time comes for all of us maybe that will help you pick up the signals and make the decision.

Be professional by

Resisting the temptation to take short-cuts.
Avoiding "backsliding."
Not giving in to peer or pupil pressure.
Knowing when to break the chain.
Diving as much as possible.
Staying fit.
Knowing when to step back from the edge.

5. Sabotaging the Dive Industry from Within

For some time now the scuba diving industry in the USA, Europe and Australia, the places where it has been longest established, has been trying to deal with a new problem. Whisper it softly but, in the parts of the world where scuba diving was traditionally strongest, the sport is becoming less popular.

Recognising the problem, training agencies have responded with a number of marketing initiatives such as asking divers to make a special effort to introduce their friends and colleagues to the sport, (something most divers do anyway) and by making it easier for people to learn to dive or have a scuba experience. However, the number of people coming into diving continues to fall.

I mention this later in the wider context of Section 5: The State of the Scuba Nation." Here I want to examine the possibility that one of the reasons that fewer people are becoming divers these days is that we who work in scuba diving, accustomed as we are to decades of growth, do not actually treat our customers very well and that is why our industry is failing in its traditional heartland. Perhaps we should be looking closely at what we do and how we act to see if the problems with diver recruitment and retention may actually be self-generated.

Failing to Close

Over the years, a number of people, many of whom are excellent swimmers with an interest in the natural world, have told me that they tried scuba diving once but found that it was not for them. On being questioned more closely they say that they felt uncomfortable, inadequate or clumsy; that it did not come naturally to them or they did not think they would make good divers.

What they are actually saying is that they were sufficiently drawn by scuba diving to pay for a course of lessons or a scuba experience and in some way the people involved with delivering that course or experience managed to put them off ever doing it again.

When these people first contacted the dive operator they were not just window shopping, they had already decided that they were interested in becoming a scuba diver. In commercial terms the initial sale, the most difficult part of any business transaction, had been made. They had purchased the product. All the dive operator then had to do was make sure they were happy with their purchase and they would continue to buy additional "products" from scuba businesses for the rest of their diving lives.

Yet somehow the dive operator contrived to ensure that their first purchase was also their last. In fact, although the operator gained financially from the transaction, they actually failed truly to close the sale.

In scuba diving, the sale is closed, not when someone signs up for a beginner's course or scuba experience, but when that person becomes a diver, when they buy their equipment, when they sign up for a diving holiday or when they sign up for further training.

If a dive centre owner or instructor thinks of sales only in terms of recruiting non-divers to take scuba try-outs or beginners' courses and not in terms of doing their utmost to ensure that these people are so thrilled by their experience of diving that they want to do it again and again, then they are sabotaging the industry that gives them their livelihood.

Deliberately Providing Poor Service

I was chatting with a dive centre manager once and I remarked on the poor condition of the rental gear that he issued to beginners. "Of course," he said, "we do it deliberately. It encourages them to buy their own equipment."

I was stunned. In one sentence, he was demonstrating a complete lack of concern for his customers and no appreciation at all of the true consequences of this policy. On a side note, he was evidently also ignorant of the fact that dive centres make much more in percentage terms from renting out equipment than they do from selling it.

His thinking is about as wrong-headed as you can get. If new divers do not enjoy the experience of diving, if they are not made comfortable and given equipment that makes diving as easy as possible for them, then there is an excellent chance that they will not pursue the sport at all. They will not become divers, they will not rent equipment again and they will certainly not buy anything!

Scuba diving competes for customers with other sports such as surfing, skiing, fishing and golf. The competition is tough enough already without us giving other sports a helping hand.

The dive centre manager is evidently not alone in thinking this way. A while ago, I was consulting for a hotel chain that was looking for a local operator to run their on-site dive centre. One applicant, a very well known company with many branches, invited me and one of the hotel chain's directors to go diving with their flagship dive centre in order to impress us. The owner of the company himself took us out.

The hotel director was a new-ish diver with sixty logged dives but did not have his own gear. "No problem," the owner said, "you can use ours." All the equipment was pretty shabby but it was the fins that were the real attention-grabbers. There was a thick white wear line where the foot pocket joined the blade and you could easily bend the blades up and down beyond 180 degrees. In the water the fins just flapped around uselessly. When we pointed this out, the owner shrugged his shoulders and blamed his non-diving customers who would wear the fins as they walked through the woods from the dive centre to the beach-snorkelling area. We were dumbstruck. He acted as if this was a valid reason for the dive centre to rent fins out to divers in this state.

I noticed that my buddy did not have a dive computer so asked if the dive centre could lend him one but the owner told us they did not have rental computers. "No need anyway," he added, "your guide has one." When I pressed the point, he explained that dive computers were expensive to replace if a customer lost one, so his policy was not to offer this service. Needless to say, the hotel chain did not give him the contract.

Try It Yourself

Instructors and dive centre owners should perhaps try out the equipment that they give beginners themselves. They should experience first hand how awkward it is and maybe then they would have some sympathy and improve the quality of their service. Those who do not make sure that every one of their divers, no matter how inexperienced, has the means to record depth, time and decompression status on every dive should reflect on how naked they would feel if they had to dive without a computer.

Making Life Difficult

Anecdotal examples abound of how, for some unfathomable reason, many dive instructors seem to put a lot of effort into making learning to dive as difficult as possible.

A lady named Sarah once told me that for her first pool session with a very large and successful dive centre in the Caribbean, she was not offered a wetsuit for her pool sessions and ended the day with knee and elbow scrapes. She also had raw patches on her shoulders where the BCD straps had chafed her skin. The BCD fitted her so badly and she was so heavily weighted that, on the surface, even when her BCD was fully inflated, her chin would still be at water level while the shoulder straps hovered above her ears.

The depth gauge on Sarah's console did not work and when she pointed this out, her instructor just said, "it doesn't matter, we are in a pool; we know how deep it is!" She cancelled the course after the first day but fortunately she did not give up. She found another dive centre and another instructor and is now a proud and certified new diver. But Sarah is the exception: we rarely get a second chance to recruit someone to our sport when we mess it up first time.

Someone who did not come back and give scuba diving another try was Dorene, a water baby of 60 who had always wanted to learn to scuba dive but had never found the time. She signed up for a course, persuaded her husband to join her then went shopping and bought a couple of thousand dollars worth of equipment from the dive centre before the course began; the large financial commitment mirroring her determination to finally become a diver.

In the pool both she and her husband managed all the skills with aplomb. They even achieved mastery of the skill sequence requiring them to remove the equipment at the deep end then surface, take a breath and descend to put it all back on again. However, on the final night the instructor asked the students to put their equipment on while standing at the side of the pool. They were to put their arms through the straps of the BCD then swing the equipment up and over their heads, slipping it on as they did so.

She tried this a couple of times, but only succeeded in banging her head with the cylinder and nearly dropping everything. As she stood there bruised and battered the instructor approached and announced none too gently that if she wanted to become a real diver, she was going to have to learn how to do this. That evening, thinking about it, she realised she just did not have the physical strength to lift that amount of weight easily over her head and decided that evidently scuba diving was not for her. Distressed and disappointed, she abandoned the course, as did her husband, and six months later they sold all their almost unused equipment at a substantial loss.

As a side note: after she called to cancel, neither the dive centre nor the instructor tried to find out why she had quit the class or invite her to try again.

No Excuses

I can just imagine the excuses that these instructors and dive centre managers would come up with if challenged on the poor treatment they mete out to customers, pleading financial and time constraints or complaining about competitors that force them to cut corners. But reflect on this, banks are hardly a benchmark for customer service these days, but even they know how important it is to look after new customers with special treatment and services. What do we do in the dive industry? Make them feel uncomfortable and unappreciated. It's a wonder any of them stick around!

Be professional by

Recognising that the customer is king (or queen.)
Doing everything in your power to give your divers the best possible experience.

6. The Sex Trap

The scene: four people are standing in a loose group next to a swimming pool at a dive resort on the edge of a white sand beach in paradise. One of them, a male scuba diving instructor, is briefing the others on skills that they will be doing in the pool in preparation for a scuba experience. The other three, two boys and a girl, all in their early twenties, are listening attentively.

Although the instructor is addressing the group, his feet and his entire body language are aimed directly at the girl. With every point he makes, she reacts, nodding and smiling. He rarely looks at the boys at all. One of the boys, the girl's partner apparently, cranes his neck towards the girl and stares with serious intent at the instructor in an attempt to get noticed and involve himself in proceedings. The other boy stands apart, ignored and excluded. It is like a scene from a teenage house party in a Hollywood movie.

When the group enter the water, the interplay continues. The girl is full of questions and needy of the instructor's assistance, the boyfriend hovers around the two of them like a satellite. The third diver floats alone most of the time.

It is common dive centre policy to use scuba experiences to sell a full beginners' course. At the end of the ocean dive, the divers are told that what they have done can count as the first lesson, confined water session and open water dive of a full course and are offered the full course at a discounted rate because they have already paid for their scuba experience. The strategy often works, especially if the divers have had a great time.

The next day the couple are again at the pool although with a different instructor, having signed up for the full beginners' course. The third diver is at the hotel reception desk, renting a bicycle to go on a tour of the island. He tells the clerk that he has had enough of diving.

The Sex Trap

Of course, there may have been other factors involved, but my guess, given the body language on display at the pool, is that the ocean dive proceeded in a similar fashion and the third diver felt anxious at being more or less left to his own devices. He did not enjoy himself and it is likely that his over-riding feeling on completing the dive was relief that he had survived. The dive centre and the sport of scuba diving as a whole lost a recruit. The boy was cheated out of becoming a diver by the instructor's poor professionalism.

The phenomenon of instructors allowing sexual attraction to influence the way they work and falling into what I call "the sex trap," can have much more serious consequences than those that befell the participants in this story. In many places, taking tourists out on try dives is big business. In Asia the majority of the customers are young ladies but there are also some boys in the groups from time to time.

Because diving is booming in the region, it is common for the in-water ratios to be very high: sometimes four or more divers to one instructor. No matter how good the instructors are, nobody on their own can adequately look after this number of non-divers underwater simultaneously and occasionally a diver will become separated from the group, get lost and drown.

Despite being in the minority, it is almost always one of the boys that dies, not because they are foolhardy and take unnecessary risks but because they are largely ignored by the predominantly male instructors and just forgotten. Often the instructors do not realise they have lost a diver until they return to shore. They are so caught up with watching, entertaining and impressing the girls that the boys are not even on their radar screen.

Wetsuits!

When I owned a dive centre in Guam, we also used to get groups of girls coming into the shop to do introductory dives and the guys on staff would get very excited by this, especially on a quiet day when they were a little bored. The shop staff would sign the girls up for the dive, do the paperwork, play the video and send them over to the instructors to choose dive gear.

I would wander over to watch what was happening and more often than not I would catch them fitting the girls out with equipment but no wetsuits. "Wetsuits!" I would say loudly.

They would glance up at me guiltily and groan but I would insist: "wetsuits!"

It was not that I thought that the guys would use the fact that the girls were in bikinis to assault them in some way. I was concerned that there should be no unnecessary distractions taking the guys' minds off their work and the over-riding duty to keep their divers safe.

My Hero!

Here is a story that illustrates another very common phenomenon. Steven, an instructor working in Florida, would often teach classes in the pool at a small hotel. As he was setting up, the hotel manageress, a lady named Linda, would often pass by and chat. Steven told her she was welcome to join in any time she liked and, after a few months watching the divers go through their paces, she asked if she could join in on the next beginners' course.

On the first morning, the group was in the pool, kneeling in the shallow end and practicing mask clearing when Linda started choking and spat her regulator out. Steven held her shoulder gently, eased the regulator back between her lips, purged it briefly to give her air to breathe and waited until she stopped spluttering and opened her eyes. He waited a little longer until her eyes lost their glaze and found their focus then he motioned with his thumb, asking her if she wanted to ascend. She nodded vigorously, remembered what she had been briefed to do and jerked her thumb up enthusiastically. Steven signalled "ascend" to the group and everyone just stood up. Linda removed her regulator and looked at Steven with an intensity that initially took him aback.

"You saved my life!" she cried, "you saved my life!"

"No, I didn't," he said. "I was just there to help. You did very well not to panic."

"Oh, my God, I thought I was going to die. You saved me! How can I ever thank you?"

She didn't continue with the course, unfortunately, but every time she met Steven in public after that, at a party or in a coffee shop, she would introduce him, with eyes glistening and a hand paced tenderly on his arm, as the man who saved her life. Each time she did this, Steven says, he would curl up inside with embarrassment as he knew it would have been more accurate if she had introduced him as the man who had failed to teach her how to dive.

Feel the Power

The thought that crossed my mind on hearing this story, a thought that has occurred to me frequently over the years in similar situations, is, "what power a scuba instructor has!" This is power that needs to be managed intelligently and sensitively and not abused or misused. After all, the power derives not from the instructor as an individual but rather from the situation in which the instructor is placed. It is important for all instructors to understand the illusory nature of the sort of emotions that can be stirred in someone by the thought that, when they were in mortal danger, they were rescued by a gallant knight or warrior princess.

As an instructor, the fact that you take people into an alien environment and bring them back alive and the fact that you look so comfortable in an environment where they feel so clumsy can enhance your appeal enormously. One of the biggest mistakes you can make is to start believing that you actually are a superhero. In the scuba diving world we try to sell a carefree, sexy lifestyle to encourage people to become divers. When this works and you find that you are suddenly more attractive than you ever were before you became an instructor, you need to be aware that this is an illusion too and it is just a matter of the industry propaganda being reflected back at you.

Guest Services

People can also misunderstand good service, courtesy and attentiveness as signs of sexual interest. It is part of our job in diving to listen to customers' long stories, to laugh at their jokes, even if we have heard them before, to admire their photographs, be impressed with their new equipment, boost their diving confidence, try to solve their problems and be there when we are needed. We make our customers feel important, as indeed they are, but when this is misunderstood as something more than a facet of our job, people sometimes respond inappropriately and this can lead to awkward situations.

Amy, a former live-aboard cruise director, tells of instances when she would hear a gentle tap on her cabin door late at night. She would go to open it and in the corridor would be one of her male customers saying something like, "um, did I read the messages you were sending me right?" She would politely send them away with a smile and an "off you go, don't be silly."

As an instructor, you need to learn to anticipate the possibility that your behaviour may be misinterpreted and deal with approaches and expressions of interest kindly but unambiguously. Developing a strategy in advance for dealing with such situations will help. Amy's tactic was effective in that it served to defuse the awkward moment quickly and avoiding any need for further discussion. Another useful tactic could be to immediately acknowledge the misunderstanding and apologise for the confusion, blaming yourself. In all circumstances, stay light-hearted, don't dwell on it and try to move on as if nothing has happened.

But This Is Why I Joined Up!

The scuba diving industry does not only target divers with lifestyle promises. As I mentioned in the chapter "Do You Have What it Takes?" the recruitment advertisements for instructors too tend to suggest a career filled with hedonistic bliss. If you are a new instructor who fell for the propaganda and are reading this thinking that, as you hoped, you are embarking on a career where you be able to translate your position into opportunities for sex, well in some respects you are right.

But if this brings a spark to your eye and makes you rub your hands together with glee, don't get too excited. Most dive operators take mixing work and play very seriously and staff who cannot tell the difference are soon shown the door. To be blunt, if you want to get paid for having sex with your customers there are other professions you can choose!

Be professional by

Identifying the potential pitfalls.
Avoiding the sex trap.
Not believing the industry propaganda.

7. Alternatives to Instruction

I thought it would be interesting to include in Scuba Professional a few contributions from people who have forged successful careers in scuba diving that do not primarily involve teaching or managing a dive centre. So I sent out a questionnaire to a select group of folk. As you will see, all were most generous in agreeing to share their experiences so that others might learn from them and perhaps be inspired by the sometimes tortuous and fortuitous paths they have trodden to get to where they are today.

I have reproduced what they wrote almost verbatim, which makes for a long chapter but allows you to hear their individual voices. The consistent themes I hear in these accounts are chance encounters, niches perceived and opportunities seized. I am sure you will be struck, as I was, by how many of the contributors parlayed skills they already had into diving careers, how much they enjoy the plusses of their working lives and how little they dwell on the minuses. Of course, this is just a tiny sample of the type of jobs available in the world of scuba diving but I hope there is enough variety here to spark the imagination.

My Job in Diving: Ian Thomas - CCR Safety Diver on Medical Research Projects

A typical workday has me up at 6 a.m. to calibrate my team's Inspiration rebreathers. Breakfast follows and, at about 8 a.m. we go in and do our dive of the day, usually a TRIMIX dive to a depth of maximum 100m (330ft.) with a run time of two to three hours. As well as the rebreather we each carry two 12l. (80 cu.ft.) bailout cylinders. We also have a system for getting additional gasses to decompressing divers in an emergency. Our dives are mostly routine but we are prepared for anything. Once we all got caught in a whirlpool with 25 minutes of decompression still to complete. During the remainder of the dive we had to concentrate intensely and manage our SMBs to try to prevent ourselves being pulled down one minute and sucked to the surface the next. By the time we surfaced we were over a mile from the reef!

Around mid-day, on return to the main boat, we eat toasted cheese and tomato sandwiches, every day! Then I clean the units, replace any batteries, cells etc. that need replacing and fill oxygen and diluent bottles. We have 50l. (212 cu.ft.) oxygen cylinders on the boat and premixed banks of TRIMIX 10/50. We use a Haskel booster pump for the gasses. At 2 p.m. I have lunch followed by a siesta if no extra gas filling is needed. At 5 p.m. I prepare the rebreathers for the following day and then spend a couple of hours exercising, listening to music and working on a series of children's novels I have been writing. Dinner is at 8 p.m. and my lights normally go out a little after 9 p.m.

I got into this line of work when I met the scientists on a Pacific atoll where I was working with a film crew shooting a documentary. I introduced them to the concept of rebreathers and TRIMIX and they called me a few months later to arrange some training. At the time I was already an IANTD TRIMIX CCR Instructor Trainer and a qualified professional diver in the UK. I had worked in the sport diving industry for a few years after retiring early from the UK police and had spent a number of years working with film crews all over the world from the Arctic to the Antarctic.

Why do I do it? Like many people I started working as a professional diver because of my passion for going underwater, a passion that has never diminished. Being married with a teenage stepdaughter, I need a pay cheque and this work provides me with a good income while at the same time giving me many of the things I love in life, such as travel, diving and exploration.

I like working with a team and I believe the research that the scientists I look after on the dives are doing is potentially extraordinarily beneficial for mankind. That is a thought that gets me up with a bounce each morning. The only drawback is being away from home for long periods of time. This is something that both you and your family have to accept.

To succeed in this type of work, you need to be a team player. You must also have the strength of character to say "No" when necessary and a touch of madness to keep going. Of course, it is essential that you understand all aspects of technical diving and have the experience to dive deep safely. Get as much experience in as many different types of diving as you can. Always put yourself forward to dive and talk to other professional divers. Build a network. That is how you learn about the opportunities available. Generally if you need to submit a CV you are not going to get the job!

I hope to keep doing this job until I eventually retire. Then I will have more time to write my children's novels.

My Job in Diving: Jen Darby (Liveaboard Adventures) Dive Travel Specialist, Agent and Tour Guide

My workdays can go two different ways. When I am in the office I start around 8 a.m. and sometimes I am still there at 10 p.m. trying to take care of all the details of guest trips including hotels, airline tickets and boat and trip descriptions. When I am leading trips I am normally up at 6 a.m. before any of the guests, so I can look at the weather and talk to the cruise directors to be sure all is well on the boat and discuss our plans for the day.

Then we start the daily liveaboard schedule of eat/dive/doze until after dinner. I normally wait for the night divers to come back and make sure all the guests are happy before heading to my cabin for the night. If we are in an area where there is Internet I have to skip a dive or two to take care of business but I can't really complain. The view from my office window is spectacular!

I started diving over 25 years ago, fell in love with it and eventually became an instructor. I wanted to be in the water constantly and living in a small town in Alabama and working in a government job were preventing me pursuing my passion. I could make only two 7-night dive trips a year. These trips were very important to me and I relied completely on the agencies who were booking my travel to be honest with me in their descriptions of resorts, liveaboards, diving etc. However, I was frequently disappointed.

The final straw came when an agent sold me on a beautiful luxury room on the water in Roatan. At the time I was unaware that such a thing did not exist. The room had no screens in the windows, the beds sagged in the middle and the shower ran cold unless you stood under it with your hand pressed on a power switch. There was no AC and with the windows open and no screens we were eaten alive by mosquitos. Also the room was not so much on the water as IN the water. It came all the way to our door at high tide and we had to wade our way to the main lodge for meals. It was that trip that convinced me that I could do it better.

I started a company specializing in Caribbean destinations and decided that truth in advertising was everything. "Been There Dived That," was my tagline and I pooled all my savings and spent time traveling to and researching major dive spots in the Caribbean and Central America. I was determined to give divers exactly what they asked for when they booked a trip. The business grew, I sold it and then spent five years selling trips to Papua New Guinea, a country where I have now spent over a year of my life and still to this day have a huge passion for. Then in 2004 I started a second company, Liveaboard Adventures, focusing on putting guests on the best liveaboards in the world. I now spend at least six months a year leading groups on custom designed trips mostly in Indonesia and Papua New Guinea. My new taglines are "Dive Your Dreams" and "Why Watch The Discovery Channel When You Can Live It."

I do this work completely out of for the passion I have for diving and traveling the world learning about other cultures and meeting people. If you are looking for money you need to look elsewhere as this is a lifestyle job. It is not a way to get rich.

To succeed in this line of business, you need a strong work ethic, be willing to work long hours, make do without holidays and be attentive to detail, as the secret to successful dive travel lies in the small things. You must be service orientated and a people person, as you will have to get on with folk who have all sorts of personalities. And have passion; without the passion you will not survive the disappointments.

My Job in Diving: John Shaw – Equipment Manufacturers Agent/Distributor and Scuba Instructor

A typical workday involves promoting products made by the manufacturers (principals) that I work with. I do shop visits; make telephone calls; promote via the Internet and social media and attend shows, exhibitions and demonstration days. Then there is the general work of running a business; invoicing, order placing, packing and shipping goods out to retail outlets.

I have been in sales all my working life and started diving in 2003. Looking to combine the two, I talked to people I knew who were already working in scuba diving and eventually landed a position as head of sales and marketing with VR Technology, a dive computer and rebreather manufacturer. When the recession hit and the company could no longer afford me, I left and started my own business, Shawtek, which would act as a sales agent for VR Technology equipment and non-competing products made by other manufacturers. It took me at least three years to source the best and most profitable manufacturers to work with and Shawtek has now evolved into a distribution company importing into the UK equipment from a number of suppliers, mainly in Poland.

For the first three years money was very tight but Shawtek is now making solid progress. Scuba divers are generally conservative, at least in the UK, and it always takes time for new products or brands to become accepted. You need perseverance, a thick skin and a never-take-no-for-an–answer attitude to succeed in a business like this. It also helps to have a supportive partner who can supplement your income in the early days.

Now I combine the business with teaching technical diving. I enjoy my lifestyle and like being my own boss and not having to answer to anyone else. I control my diary and decide who I see and when I see them. Money is still something of an issue. If it were not, I would be travelling and diving around the world instead of teaching a TRIMIX rebreather class in an English quarry. But the business is growing and I am always on the lookout for new products. However, anything I take on now has to offer something new or possess a unique selling point. I am not interested in copies of equipment that is already on the market. At some point in the near future, the business will become too much for one person to operate and then I will take on staff.

If I could give one piece of advice to someone wanting to follow me into this line of work, it would be, "don't promote anything if you can't make money from it." When I first started I was so desperate to have something to sell that I accepted anything. Often I would make a sale and by the time I had factored in the cost of the petrol I used to deliver it, the profit I had "earned" had evaporated into thin air!

My Job in Diving: Kristine Hobson – Liveaboard Cruise Director, Indonesia

In my job I usually wake up in a different place every day! After surfacing from below decks, the first thing I see is a new ocean view. It may be a white sand beach in Tual, karst rock formations in Raja Ampat or a beautiful reef-trimmed atoll lagoon in Maratua. It is magical to watch the sun rise over locations like these. Notice that I said "rise?" That's right, I am usually up around 6.15 a.m. We make sure that first breakfast is ready for our guests to give them the fuel to set them off on the fun filled day of diving ahead. Our first dive usually begins around 8:00 a.m.; followed by second breakfast; followed by a second dive; followed by lunch; followed by a little personal time; followed by a third dive; followed by a snack. Are you noticing a pattern here? Then our night dive is followed by dinner, a little chit chatting with the guests and, finally, bed. I fall into unconsciousness for a couple hours and, on a good night, I dream about what I may be lucky enough to see underwater the next day.

I did not always work as a liveaboard cruise director. I previously owned a bar and restaurant in the Caribbean and was pretty much land bound, sleeping or doing the books during the day and working at night. After five years of this, I realized I hadn't moved to the Caribbean just to work and sleep, so I did something about it and got in the water. Within two years I had worked my way up to a divemaster qualification and had sold the business. My boyfriend was a scuba instructor and friends who worked in scuba diving contacted us and told us about a liveaboard dive boat in Indonesia that was looking for a second set of cruise directors. We thought, "why not? Let's give it a try."

What are the benefits? I get to do what I love. I am still amazed daily by the marine life we see in Indonesia. I also like the liveaboard life style. It's a set schedule, but because most divers are laidback and easy-going it's not too regimented. I usually eat pretty well and exercise by diving three or four times a day. (I love current!) Because the areas we travel through are so remote, I have nowhere to spend the money I earn, so when I get some time off the boat I have usually saved enough to take a nice dive vacation.

Of course, the remoteness can be a drawback as you are far away from family and friends. You work long hours and if you like to get a little time for yourself now and then, forget about it. You can't afford to get sick, even in a minor way, as it is very difficult to bring in a replacement and the last thing you want to do is get your guests sick.

To succeed in a job like this, you need flexibility, patience, an outgoing personality and a sense of propriety. You have to be able to make the tough decisions. You and the boat captain are responsible for the safety and comfort of all the guests and crew and, whenever you are at sea, you have to put their safety above all else.

If you are thinking that this sounds perfect for you – go for it! It's the best experience I have ever had. But I would offer one piece of advice. Always remember that the boat is not a democracy. You and the captain are the experts and the leaders. You need to be strong, firm in your decisions and always take into account the feelings, interests, strengths and weaknesses of EVERYONE on board. Never let someone bully you into doing something that you feel is not safe for the boat, the guests, the crew or you.

My Job in Diving: Peter Symes - Editor-in-chief and publisher (X-Ray International Magazine & AquaScope Media)

Mine is largely an office job interspersed with travel to dive shows and events, a little fieldwork and the odd dive trip. On an average morning, I start off by revisiting plans, schedules and appointments and re-evaluating my priorities for the day, the week and further ahead. I compartmentalise everything and deal with one or two matters at a time, focusing on the tasks in hand and getting them completed before moving on to the next.   While doing this, I do not check emails, text messages or social media. I check these at specific times during the day; otherwise I fear I would get nothing important done. After lunch most days I focus on editorial matters and sales. In the evenings I do creative work, develop our IT and enjoy a wee bit of peace and quiet.

I have a graduate degree in biology specialising in aquatic ecology and have always been drawn to life sciences foremost as a scientist and explorer. I also majored in media & communications, which I always considered   secondary to biology in my list of priorities. To this day, decades after leaving academia, I feel I am a scientist first and foremost and a communicator second.

I did my first dive training while still in university. It was not part of the curriculum. I just went to a local dive club and became a member. I was motivated partly because I saw it as a natural and integral part of a future career and also partly because I was attracted and intrigued by the sport on a personal level. I was keen to do more diving but it was not until I was in my late 20s that I could actually afford it. The sport was too expensive for a poor student! I stayed involved by assisting as a volunteer with some dive industry events and offered to help with the sport diving federation magazine.

In one way that is how it all started. After obtaining my masters degree, I spent about five years trying to get enough research grants together to do a Ph.D. but, eventually, having a growing family to take care of, I realised I had to pursue a different path and used the dive industry contacts I had made to cross the threshold into diving as a career. Running a dive magazine and working with dive media and travel has enabled me to pursue my interest in aquatic environments while making a living but I confess I do often miss being an researcher.

Every day, I take a great deal of pride in having built the brand from scratch, achieved our goals and implemented the original vision with no support or outside funding. We not only prevailed in the face of adversity and widespread scepticism, we also kept on expanding during difficult times when both media and diving were contracting and the world economy was going through hard times.

The work has allowed me to meet many remarkable people; scientists, explorers, naturalists, artists, photographers, entrepreneurs and visionaries, many of whom are now close friends. I have also had the good fortune to see some stunning places on this planet and be blessed with amazing encounters with wildlife underwater. It is a source of great satisfaction to know that there is probably no place on the planet I cannot go and visit if I really want to.

Success has come at the price of very long hours and constant worries about money and the future. Working in the dive industry, you have to contend with big egos and personality conflicts. As a business manager I loathe the burden of constantly having to deal with delinquent debtors and mismanaged accounts. The frequent negativity and barefaced nastiness that you are often faced with are not for the faint of heart. To survive, you need tenacity and a clear vision coupled with a sound business plan. You also need to be able to handle stress, make decisions under duress as well as be prepared to make the tough and painful calls in a timely way.

If you are thinking of this line of work, you must appreciate that you are running a business and that the dive industry is not just a playground for living out fanciful daydreams. Your business needs to be profitable. If you cannot balance your accounts you will not last long. Plan on it taking at least twice as long to succeed as you expected and count on expenses being double those you anticipated. Be very frugal and hold off on any investments and expenses that are not entirely necessary until revenue really starts to build. In addition to formal training in business management, I suggest you watch episodes of Gordon Ramsay's Kitchen Nightmares, as the dysfunctional restaurants therein seem to have quite a few parallels in the scuba diving industry. You will find yourself dealing with plenty of dreamers with little commercial acumen.

My plan now is to strive to stay on top of our game, not resting on our laurels but always evolving. I have several ideas for expanding our business, which could keep us busy for some time yet. The key for future success is to keep an open mind and not be tied to dogma. New opportunities sometimes knock very subtly so I intend to keep listening intently.

My Job in Diving: Tim Rock – Underwater Photojournalist

It all started while I was on R&R from the Vietnam War. I had a week's leave in Thailand and was determined to make the most of it. Even more determined was the guy sitting next to me on the flight from Saigon to Bangkok. He was stationed at a Hellhole, a firebase on the Cambodian border. There the threat of attack was ever-present. He told me he knew how to dive, said he would "teach" me and asked if I would like to join him. After a day or two of debauchery, we headed south to a quiet fishing area with a stunning beach called Pattaya to try this scuba thing.

I grew up next to a lake but I was not prepared for what I saw. The colours of the reef blew me away. Angelfish swirled around castles and cities of coral. I was completely hooked. To top it off, our new girlfriends had taken the boat over to an island and bought lunch. When we came out of the water and up the ladder on the boat, they greeted us, led us to lounge chairs, towelled us off, sat on our laps and fed us fresh fruits and fish. What a great sport I had just discovered! Thousands of dives later, I am still waiting for the after dive pampering to happen again: but I digress.

The path I took to my eventual career was more coincidental than purposeful. I attended the University of Nebraska-Omaha journalism program and embarked on a career in television news broadcasting, concentrating on learning the skills that would make me a competent and in-demand broadcast photojournalist.

Unsurprisingly, the memory of the two dives in Thailand never left me and eventually I found myself taking snorkelling vacations to the Mexican Yucatan peninsula and experimenting with taking underwater photos, having borrowed a Nikonos II camera that I had purchased in Vietnam for my brother. A talented young local photographer named Tom Langdon had just ventured into a new medium called Cibachrome and could print my slides. We took diving lessons together, bought a catamaran and dived around the US Midwest.

Four seminal moments followed. The first came when Skin Diver Magazine published an article I had submitted and I signed up with Tom to give presentations at the Our World Underwater dive show in Chicago. Buoyed by this success I was ready for seminal moment number two.

I was aware that, to make progress in this burgeoning second career I had to live somewhere where the diving opportunities were better than in the Midwest. I scoured Broadcast Magazine for jobs and found news photographer jobs in Bermuda, the US Virgin Islands and Guam. It turned out that only Guam had the sort of state-of-the-art quality video equipment I was used to working with. So I went to Guam. Everyone I met there, it seemed, was a diver. I bought a boat and, together with some of my new colleagues, went diving: a lot! I started doing weekly segments on the world of the sea for local television and also edited a Sunday magazine, which helped me hone my writing and still photography skills.

Seminal moment three was about to arrive. I noticed that there were no diving guidebooks that covered Guam, Truk Lagoon, Palau or any of the islands of Micronesia. With the help of local publisher Lee Webber, I produced Guam's first diving guide and established a book company called Marine Images. Chapters for Rota, Saipan, Tinian, Palau, Yap and Truk Lagoon soon followed and then further chapters on the dive sites of Papua New Guinea, Bali and the Philippines: then a separate Bali book.

This major Pacific collective book caught the eye of a Texas publisher who produced the internationally distributed Pisces diving guides. I signed a contract with him to do a Micronesia series and, when the Lonely Planet folk subsequently bought out Pisces, I remade the books for them. Eventually I was to write over a dozen Lonely Planet guides. The final element that persuaded me to give up my day job and start working in diving full time was the success of a regional television series called Aquaquest Micronesia that I co-produced using my former broadcasting skills.

Seminal moment four occurred while I was developing my new career. It occurred during my divemaster training. I was taking some newly certified divers on a shallow dive. Of course, divemasters must have their hands free during a working dive to take care of any problems that arise, so I did not have my camera with me. During that dive I showed four novice divers a seahorse, a rare lionfish and three or four other normally hard-to-find Guam creatures. Being new, they may have had no idea that they had just been on a pretty special dive. But I knew it.

I hurried home, grabbed my camera and a fresh tank, went back to the site, jumped in and completely failed to find any of the creatures I had seen just an hour before. It was right then that I realized I had to make a decision. That was: teach or shoot? I quit instructor training and concentrated on the reason I moved to the Pacific: photography. Ever since, for over thirty years, I have never made a dive without a camera in hand.

Today I have over fifty books to my name and have produced a couple of different television series. I have six photo agents and two story/image agents. I am a correspondent for six magazines and write product reviews online. I even blog a bit. I have postcards, posters and art in hospitals and galleries and am now publishing yet another new series of dive guides.

Am I living the dream? Well, at least I am living my dream. But every day I have to work hard to keep the dream alive. I take no days off. This profession has been very good to me but it has to be continuously nurtured.

So Ya Wanna Be an Underwater Photographer?

1. Get a journalism degree. If you do, you will be one of very few qualified professionals in the diving world and your

training in how to deal with editors and publishers and meet deadlines will put you well ahead of the competition.

2. Know the technical side of your trade.

3. Hire a good business manager or agent. If you want to shoot, you need to be out in the field, not sitting behind a desk.

4. Learn the language of contracts, copyright law and the business side of things. Having talent and working hard is good but you must also be a decent businessperson to be successful.

5. Seek out lucrative magazine or video contracts. There are many more magazines outside the dive industry than within and they pay much better.

6. Never give anything away for free.

7. Have a thick skin. Even established pros get their story ideas turned down. Don't let a few refusals discourage you.

8. Before you pitch editors, read their magazine and identify the magazine's style and verve. This will make sure you don't suggest material that they would never run.

9. Be entrepreneurial. The things you write and the images you take can be used and re-used in many ways. You are only limited by your imagination.

10. Always be fair and honest. Your integrity is your greatest asset.

Be professional by

Spotting opportunities.
Taking chances.
Adapting the skills you already possess.

§2

Instruction

8. Remember the Days Before You Were a Diver?

When you work in an environment where almost everyone you meet is a diver, it is easy to fall into the trap of assuming that the whole world understands the concepts and language of scuba diving.

However, we occupy a small niche; the things we do are not common knowledge. You see evidence of this every time you read a story in the media that talks about divers breathing "oxygen" or watch science fiction movies where divers use machines that look like rebreathers but have streams of bubbles pouring out of them. I once asked a friend who had worked as the diving consultant on one of these movies about this and he said, "I told them it was wrong but they said that the audience would expect divers to blow bubbles. So they had to blow bubbles."

Sometimes, the misconceptions and irrational fears about scuba diving harboured by non-divers can be unnecessary obstacles preventing them from taking up the sport.

Panic in the Shower

A few years ago, a friend who was always saying that she wanted to join one of my beginners' courses called me and said, "I woke up this morning and told myself today's the day I am going to learn to dive." "Great!" I said. "The trouble is,' she continued, " I then went to have a shower and while I was in there, I turned my face up into the spray and immediately started to panic. If I can't have a shower without freaking out, how can I ever scuba dive."

I explained that the reason she had panicked was that she had held her breath when she turned her face into the shower and that our central nervous system is programmed to induce anxiety when we stop breathing. On the contrary, I told her, in scuba diving you don't hold your breath underwater at all.

I added that this was not to say that she would never become anxious underwater, but the fact that she had started to panic in the shower was completely irrelevant to the issue of whether she could become a scuba diver.

Eventually she took the course, loved it, as deep down she always knew she would, and she is now an enthusiastic diver.

Separating the Truth from the Myth

Of course, not everyone can scuba dive. There are some people who cannot dive for medical reasons. Either they have physical challenges that mean that they cannot safely breathe air under pressure and cope with substantial pressure changes or they suffer from other conditions that make it inadvisable for them to be subjected to potentially stressful situations.

But, as I said, many of the reasons that non-divers give for not scuba diving are just based on common misconceptions. Some are cultural myths exaggerated by media hysteria. Others are merely figments of the imagination. Many people who would love to learn to scuba dive, like my friend who panicked in the shower, believe you need special qualities to scuba dive or their imagination conjures up risks that don't actually exist or are mitigated by training.

Below, I list a number of the common things people come up with and suggest a few things you as an instructor can say in response to counter their objections. However, first I should emphasise that, to quote a Buddhist proverb, "when the student is ready, the master appears." Before someone learns to scuba dive, they must genuinely want to scuba dive. Whether they are driven by curiosity, spurred on by the adventure or simply want to dive in order to share the experience with friends, family or a diving spouse, the will to dive has to come from the new diver himself or herself.

It is wrong for an instructor, dive centre owner or anyone else to use persuasive arguments and force of personality to try to induce someone to dive against their will. The responses below are designed to combat false assumptions on the part of someone who wants to learn to dive. They are not arguments to be used to bully someone who really does not want to dive into trying it.

I want to learn to scuba dive but ...

I can't swim very well.

Response: a great way to prepare for a scuba diving course is to spend time swimming to improve your stamina and confidence in the water. If you are worried that you may not be able to swim well enough, then a few lessons would be a good investment. Certification agencies usually require that you can swim between 50m and 200m (165 to 660ft.) wearing just a swimsuit and float unaided for 10 minutes. These are minimum requirements.

The equipment that you wear when you scuba dive is designed to help you be more comfortable and swim more efficiently; but you should not be completely dependent on the equipment to keep you afloat. Also, the better you can swim and the happier you are in the water, the easier it will be for you to concentrate on the scuba diving skills.

I am frightened of sharks.

Response: thanks in great part to "if it bleeds, it leads" journalism, sharks have a bad reputation that is completely undeserved. The sharks you see when you scuba dive usually keep their distance from you. After all, from their perspective you are a strange, noisy, one-eyed bubbling monster and every instinct tells them to steer clear. A shark attack on a scuba diver is extremely rare. Statistics suggest you have a better chance of being killed by a cow!

I understand about sharks but there are other things down there that can hurt me.

Response: there are, and they are often small and difficult to see things such as blue-ringed octopus and scorpion fish. But they will not touch you if you do not touch them and one of the golden rules for divers is "don't mess around with the marine life!"

I've heard about the "bends;" it sounds dangerous.

Response: the bends, or decompression illness, is a risk for scuba divers but one of the main purposes of diver training is to show you how to dive in such a way as to minimise the risk. Current established safe diving procedures are very effective at protecting divers from the bends.

I am afraid my ears will hurt.

Response: one of the first things you will be taught in your diving course is how to equalise the pressure in your body's air spaces (lungs, ears, sinuses etc.) with the surrounding water pressure, usually by squeezing your nostrils together and blowing against a closed nose. You have probably done this before in an aircraft when you are coming into land and the captain increases the air pressure in the cabin.

I don't like to wear anything over my face.

Response: many people feel like this but your mask is an essential part of your scuba diving equipment. Without it you cannot see very well and you cannot equalise. It doesn't take long to get used to it. After all it's not that much different from wearing big sunglasses!

I worry I won't be good at it.

Response: the fact that you are concerned about this is actually a good sign. A very healthy attitude to have when embarking on any new activity is a slight fear of failure. It raises your adrenalin, it heightens your level of attentiveness and it makes you try harder. This is something instructors actually like to see in their students when they start: it means they are more likely to succeed than someone who comes to class complacent, thinking it is all going to be easy.

I can't imagine breathing underwater; it's unnatural.

Response: yes, it is unnatural. We are terrestrial mammals for goodness sake! But you will be amazed how curiously natural it all feels just a few minutes into your first dive when you are distracted by all the fish, the feeling of weightlessness, the ability to move around effortlessly in three dimensions and the thrill of entering a whole new world.

Communicating with Non-Divers

When someone starts learning to drive a car, they have a good idea of what they are going to do during the lessons. After all, they have probably been watching other people drive them around as a passenger all their life. Also, many people they know have done driving lessons and can explain to them what to expect in clear, easily understandable language.

But when someone embarks on a scuba diving course, they really do enter a whole new world. It is unlikely that they have spent any time at all watching divers do their thing. They may have friends who are already divers but, when they ask them about the course, the chances are that their explanations will be liberally littered with incomprehensible jargon such as regulator, valve and narcosis and bizarre acronyms like BCD, SPG and NDL.

Yes, it is true, after they have done a couple of training dives they will be discussing such opaque (to the uninitiated) concepts as equalizing, mask clearing, neutral buoyancy, air sharing and back-rolling with other divers as if they have been one of the scuba in-crowd for years but before they start diving, when they are still on the outside looking in, it is all a bit bewildering.

Which is where you, the dive professional, come in. Your job is to explain to people what they will be doing on their first diving course in layman's terms and without lapsing into obscure references and concepts.

This is not as easy as it may sound. It is sometimes difficult to remember which words and phrases are commonly used in the world of non-divers and which are just diver jargon. For example, I have a friend who once put a sign outside her dive store that advertised "free-diving and yoga." Every day she would fend off folk who came into her shop looking for courses free of charge.

When you speak to non-divers and very new divers, make an effort to express diving concepts in layman's terms in order to communicate clearly and avoid both confusing and alienating them. This is something that instructor development programmes invariably get wrong. Instructor candidates are taught to speak to their students in the jargon of the sport and the specific training agency. For instance, they will say, "today we will do mask removal and replacement" rather than "today I'll show you how to put your mask back on underwater if it comes off" or "now we will do air depletion" rather than "now we will practice sharing air with another diver if you run out of air."

During the instructor training, the candidates are of course addressing other instructor candidates so everyone knows what they are talking about and scuba and agency jargon offer useful linguistic shortcuts. However, when use of this language continues beyond the instructor course, it becomes an obstacle to effective communication. New students will often have no idea what you are talking about.

Avoid this trap by always being conscious of the language you are using and the effect what you are saying has on the people you are speaking to. Match your language with the knowledge base of your audience, be alert to their reactions and be prepared to adapt the words you use. For example, when speaking to non-divers, you can refer to problem solving exercises rather than "skills," talk in terms of a pool, lake or beach rather than "confined water," even use the word flippers instead of "fins" if it helps you get your message across! After all, flippers is the word everyone uses. Nobody knows what "fins" are until they learn to dive.

There are a whole host of other examples. Putting yourself in the mind of the person you are talking to is a key step in mastering the art of communication. It may be difficult to remember what it is like not to be a diver but, if you can go back in your mind to those days, you will be better able to understand and empathise with your students and you will be a better instructor because of it.

Be professional by

Understanding how non-divers feel about scuba diving.
Knowing what to say to counter their fears.
Communicating effectively.

9. It All Comes Down to Me

As a scuba instructor, there will be many times when you find yourself inwardly cursing your students. When they fail to perform a skill properly; when they forget something you have told them a dozen times; when they flutter their arms about pointlessly whenever they are close to the sea bed; when they just don't "get it." Every time this happens, just remember this little maxim, "It all comes down to me!"

Instead of blaming the students, examine yourself. If students cannot learn quickly enough or if they forget things, this is down to you. It is your fault. Either you have not taught them well enough or the way you have arranged the session or set the course structure has presented an obstacle to learning that you and they have not been able to overcome.

Especially if you are teaching absolute beginners, it is vitally important that you deliver the very best course that you can. You are responsible for turning them into good divers who will love the sport and make diving part of their lives forever. The habits you teach them can stand them in good stead for always.

This is not your only responsibility. You are also responsible to the world of scuba diving as a whole, which provides you with a livelihood and depends upon you to provide it with more adherents.

In Pursuit of Excellence

There are a number of ways to ensure that your courses produce good divers. This is not an exhaustive list by any means but here are a lucky 13 things that have worked for me over the years.

1. Always Follow the Five Steps

In a beginners' course, many of the things we teach are survival skills. The acquisition of these skills is what gives new divers confidence and helps them conquer their fears. Each time you introduce a survival skill, you should take your students through a five-step process. First, you introduce the threat to their survival, for instance running out of air or panicking after getting water in their mask. Second, you tell them how they can deal with the threat and thereby survive. Third, you show them what to do. Fourth, you teach them how to do it themselves and fifth, you get them to practice until they can do it autonomously, automatically and effortlessly. Look for the "aha" moment that tells you the student has "got it." This will usually come during steps 2 and 3, making step 4 much easier.

The need to survive is a highly motivating force. Once students grasp that this is why they have to learn something, you can be sure that you will not only have their full attention but that they will do everything in their power to learn it well and remember it.

There is no viable short cut to the five steps. However, in fast track beginner courses, some instructors skip steps in an effort to save time. The steps they usually omit are steps one, two and five. They don't tell their students why the skill is important, they just show them what to do, watch them do it once, then move on. It is a meaningless exercise. These instructors are not teaching, they are just running through a list in their head.

This is why so many new divers still have problems with basic survival skills after their beginners' training. The reason why they need to master them was inadequately explained, so they did not attach importance to them. Nor did the students have an opportunity to practice in class, beyond demonstrating that they could mimic the skill on one occasion.

2. Create Easy Transitions

All new divers must be able to swim before they start the course but many will not be frequent swimmers or used to being in the water. Some may only go into a pool or the sea on their annual summer vacation. Many will never have worn a wetsuit before. Putting them in full scuba gear before they have even got their feet wet may therefore generate unnecessary levels of anxiety and start the course off on the wrong foot. New divers need first to feel comfortable and safe in the water. Only then will they be in the frame of mind to learn. So you need to create easy transitions to take them gently from their hitherto solely land-based existence to a future where much of their life will be spent in the water.

The original scuba diver courses began with a series of swims and buoyancy exercises without wetsuits or equipment. Students were then given snorkelling gear and shown how to use this before making the transition to scuba and wetsuits. This meant that by the time they got to use the more complex equipment, with all its awkwardness and restrictions, they were well used to being in the water and could focus on all the new information they were receiving.

Today's beginners' courses may be much shorter than in the past but the three elements, swim, snorkel and scuba, are still there and can be scheduled to make new students as relaxed as possible. During the swimming session, students can be encouraged to swim underwater holding their breath, which is an excellent mini skill to prepare them for mask exercises and the no mask swim on scuba. If a student has mastered the giant stride entry in snorkelling equipment, then doing the same in scuba gear will be much more straightforward. Other examples abound: instructors just need to use their imagination. This concept fits very well with the standard diver training philosophy that skills are learned faster and perfected more easily if they are preceded by smaller, less arduous skills.

3. Build Habits

This goes back to the fifth step in skill acquisition I mentioned above. Focus your water sessions on building habits. If you require your divers to perform skills over and over again and practice them so much that they never forget them, they will thank you and the people who dive with them and teach them in future will thank you too.

Doing the same things time after time builds conditioned responses and these can save a diver's life. Underwater, it is very hard for divers to reason their way out of an emergency as time pressure, narcosis and carbon dioxide build up interfere with their decision making processes. This can lead to them making the wrong choices and not surviving. If, on the other hand, divers have practiced self-rescue drills to the point where the skills have become instinctive, in an emergency divers will choose the correct solution automatically and have a much better chance of survival.

4. Allow Time for Reflection

You cannot assume that just because people have been exposed to a piece of information once, they will consequently understand it, remember it and be able to apply it. You have to teach it, repeat it a number of times and in different ways and then, crucially, allow your students time to think about it.

Often, something that you have found difficult to grasp one day becomes straightforward after you have mulled it over in your mind for a while or "slept on it." One reason that fast track beginners' courses are less effective is that they allow hardly any time for reflection. There is little opportunity for students to step back from the class to review a setback, such as failing to perform a skill well. There is no time for them to suppress any negative feelings, let the positives from the day surface and build determination to return to class, try it again and do better. So, if you have to teach courses quickly, introduce mini-breaks into the schedule to give students time to reflect, explaining to them what you are doing and why.

5. Identify and Pre-empt Learning Obstacles

Anticipate likely barriers to learning and ensure you organise things so that you avoid them. If barriers arise, have the discipline to dismantle them quickly and have the self-awareness to be able to spot occasions when it is actually you the instructor who are creating the barrier.

Let me explain what I mean by barriers to learning by giving a few examples.

a) Cold

If divers are cold they cannot think clearly and they will not learn. Do not put divers in the water until they have to be there. Brief and debrief in the dry and do not waste water time with talking. Keep the session moving and always give students on scuba adequate thermal protection, in pools as well as in open water.

b) Poor Quality Equipment

I raised this point earlier in the chapter "Sabotaging the Dive Industry from Within." Inadequate and poorly fitting equipment has an adverse effect on learning because it distracts students and generates stress. Do not give students poor quality, cheap rental equipment that even an experienced diver would feel awkward using.

c) Time Pressure

Students have enough to think about without becoming victims of the time pressure that instructors always have looming at the edge of their mind when teaching a course. This time pressure is yours so keep it to yourself. Always be alert for signs of student anxiety caused by the pace you are setting in order to keep up with your schedule and be prepared to take a break or change the activity if you detect that the students are flagging. Persevering with your schedule in the face of student stress or fatigue will accomplish nothing but create resentful, discontented students who have stopped listening to you and therefore stopped learning.

d) Ego

Your own ego can be a barrier to student learning. Your defects as an instructor may be difficult to perceive yourself and this is one of the reasons why asking another instructor to peer review you as you teach can be a great idea. Instructors almost always work alone and another instructor will often spot bad habits that you cannot see.

Your ego can also persuade you to avoid situations where you might not succeed. For instance, you will see many instructors pass problem students off to assistants to work with, while they stay with the group. It is the easier option and neatly sidesteps the possibility that the instructor might fail and lose prestige. In fact, it is the student in difficulty who needs the experienced instructor, not the other divers who are getting everything right first time. Much better to have the assistants review previous skills with the group while you concentrate on the person who really needs you. Anyone can tell a gifted individual what to do and then watch on while he does it right first time, every time. It takes a good instructor to teach people to dive who could never have managed it on their own. If your ego is going to intervene, let it steer you towards challenges to your talents, rather than away from them.

e) Personality Clash

Again, this is a barrier to learning for you to dismantle as soon as it appears. Every so often, you will encounter a student who you just do not like as a person. When this happens you have to remind yourself that your personal feelings about the students you teach are completely irrelevant to the process.

You have to be professional and treat all students equally. If you allow your sentiments to intrude this may have an adverse impact in terms of your effectiveness as a teacher on the group as a whole. Naturally the same applies if you find yourself attracted to one of your students, a problem I discussed in detail in the chapter "The Sex Trap."

6. Teach Defensive Diving

To be a safe motor vehicle driver you have to learn how to reduce risk by anticipating dangerous situations, taking into account adverse conditions and the actions of other drivers. This process is called defensive driving.

Right from the start teach your students to dive just as they would drive, watching the ocean as they watch the road, observing other divers in the same way as they would watch out for other drivers.

Teach them why and how diving accidents occur so they know what to avoid. Teach them how to use their knowledge to recognise when a problem is developing or when a situation has danger written all over it.

To quote an example, in the chapter "Drift Diving Disasters and How to Avoid Them," I discuss an incident where divers lost their lives on a drift dive in bad weather that went horribly wrong. Had these divers been trained in defensive diving, they could have asked questions before the dive that might have identified in advance the errors the operators were making and chosen not to do the dive. Questions might have included: -

1. What is the dive plan?

2. Who on the boat will be watching for my surface marker buoy (SMB) if I surface early?

3. Where will the boat be during our dive?

4. What emergency equipment are our guides carrying in case the boat is not there when we come up?

7. Incorporate Stress Management Drills

Every instructor must understand how people make decisions under stress and new divers need to be able to identify how and when stressful situations can take place, know that stress is a risk factor to be managed and practice ways to manage it. This topic is covered in detail in the chapter, "Detecting and Dealing with Stress."

8. Use Realistic Scenarios

Teach skills and drills and procedures that are representative of and reflect real life diving situations. Even in swimming pool environments, with a little imagination you can create realistic scenarios. For instance, you can rope off an area at the side of the pool to give students an idea of what it is like to prepare for a dive in the sort of confined space that a dive boat deck offers. Then run the pool dive with all the elements of an ocean dive, including equipment assembly, briefing, entry, waypoints, exit, debrief and cylinder changeover. Even offer refreshments!

One of the things that instructors do that does not in any way reflect the experience of scuba diving is teach the students to perform skills while they are kneeling. Yes, it is very convenient from a people-management point of view to have students static and negatively weighted. It is also very difficult for a student to bolt to the surface quickly from a kneeling position so you and your assistants have more time to intervene if a student starts to become anxious.

However, your convenience should not really be the priority. If the students are weighted so they are neutrally buoyant and if they are almost horizontal, fins touching the bottom, they can still see you demonstrate the skills, they can still practice the skills in this position and, from a safety point of view, it is even less easy for them to bolt than when they are kneeling. Yes, your assistants may have to work a little harder to help the odd student that loses control of their buoyancy and floats up but the benefit to the students is enormous. First, they are spending time underwater in the sort of position they will be in most of the time when they dive. Secondly, there is typically a lot of waiting around during the skills phase of diver training, while the instructor and assistants are taking care of other students. If they are negative and kneeling, the other students are just wasting time. If they are neutral and horizontal they are using the time practicing buoyancy control.

Apart from making a key teaching point, another reason I raise this particular issue here is to highlight the efforts of a small group of younger dive instructors who felt so strongly about the benefits teaching diving skills to students while they were horizontal and neutral rather than kneeling and negative that they petitioned their training agency, one of the major players, to change its policy and allow this. They succeeded, in spite of considerable opposition from conservative elements in the industry, and generations of future scuba students will benefit from their efforts.

So if your training agency requires that you teach a skill in away that you feel does not reflect a real life diving situation and could be improved upon, raise the issue with a more experienced instructor or trainer first and if you are still not satisfied with the answer, challenge the agency directly. People and institutions, especially large organisations, get set in their ways and institutional resistance is a common problem but no system is so good that it can't be improved. It really does all come down to you. You CAN make a difference.

9. Don't Encourage Dependency

Instructors get used to students depending on them. Many actually grow to like the feeling! However, while dependency may give a boost to the instructor's ego, it is not at all good for the student. Why? Because the instructor will not be around when the student goes diving after the course is over. By the time they graduate, all students should be able to dive independently at the level of their training with other divers of similar ability. The aim of every course, therefore, should be to take the students to the point where the instructor is no longer required. This means that, on the final dive of the course, the graduation dive, the instructor's primary role is merely to observe and debrief. If the students are still dependent in any way on the instructor's presence to execute the dive successfully then they are not ready to graduate.

10. Complete the Job

If the students have not reached the required level on the final dive of a course then you must have the strength of purpose to continue their training beyond the designated class timescale. Rather than just hand the students their certification cards, pose for photos and consign them to an uncertain future, tactfully suggest instead that they sign up for a couple more dives in your company first to "perfect their skills" or "get really comfortable." The students will rarely object. Generally speaking, they know how able they are.

I once came across a dive centre in Thailand that had adopted an elegant solution for the "not enough time" dilemma. They taught fast-track beginners' courses but included in the price two extra days of fun diving post graduation. Even though this meant the dive centre's courses were a little more expensive than those of its competitors, they still attracted a lot of customers, who perceived good value for money in the deal. Of course, not only did the two extra dive days give those who had passed the course within the allotted time some valuable additional diving experience, they also gave the instructors more teaching time with students for whom the standard course length had proven insufficient.

11. Review and Assess

After you complete a course, take time to review everything. Look for things you could have done better. If you work under time restrictions, examine particularly how efficiently you used the time at your disposal. If you had students who had difficulty with elements of the course, try to identify any barriers to learning that might have been responsible. Never be satisfied. Always take the attitude that you will never teach the perfect training course and there are always areas where you can improve.

12. Think Outside the Box

Sometimes you will need to be creative to get the job done. Training agency guidelines are designed to deal with issues that students typically have, but you will sometimes encounter situations that your training has not prepared you for and that your manuals do not cover. Read widely; there are a lot of books on scuba diving out there and it is always useful to look through other agencies' course materials. They usually do not vary much but you may find inspiration. Often, the secret to teaching a student who is having difficulty mastering a particular skill is simply to come at the problem from a slightly different angle.

Or ask another instructor for help. Do not be afraid to let your ego trump professional ethics. Sometimes just a different face with a different style of teaching will overcome the obstacle. Do whatever you need to get the job done. You owe that to your student, the person who has paid you for the course, and you owe it to yourself to maintain high standards of service and integrity.

13. Be a Team Player

Although instructors mostly work alone or with junior assistants, they are rarely autonomous. They will usually work through or for a dive operation that supplies most of the instructor's students and therefore has a significant say in how a course is conducted. In a perfect world your goals as the instructor will match those of the dive operation but this is unlikely to happen without trust, understanding and respect on both sides. This often takes time and a considerable degree of diplomacy to achieve.

Differences between dive operations and instructors usually revolve around time and money. A successful partnership is more likely if an instructor understands that the dive operation needs to make money and tailors courses with this in mind and if the operation understands that good, conscientious training fosters customer retention and a good reputation brings in more customers. Professional responsibility does not necessarily conflict with commercial gain.

Be professional by

Remembering that it all comes down to you!

10. Technical Training: It's not just Beasting

In the early days of recreational scuba diver training, many of the instructors were retired ex-military men and there was lots of talk of "beasting" and similar epithets that an instructor would use to describe the harsh regime he meted out to his students to ensure they met his exacting standards for diver certification. Much was made of dropout and failure rates, as if the quality of an instructor resided not in how many students passed his courses but how many failed.

This kind of mind-set was unlikely to build a successful commercial industry and, in the early 1960s, scuba diver training attitudes changed, led primarily by the folk who started PADI, still the way (most of) the world learns to dive.

The old attitudes still survive today, unfortunately. In the chapter "Sabotaging the Dive Industry from Within" I told the story of a lady in her sixties, a strong swimmer all her life, who signed up for a course to fulfil a long-held ambition to learn to dive but subsequently withdrew from the course after her instructor insisted that, in order to proceed, she had to be able to put her gear on by putting her arms through the BCD straps and swinging it over her head.

The Pendulum Swings

However, generally speaking, scuba diver training became much less of a commando exercise. The drills and skills changed so that they were no longer a test of courage, self-discipline, determination and the ability to conquer fear. The skills that were retained from the old military-style training were those that taught new divers how to deal with the aquatic environment, manage their equipment and rescue themselves and their buddy from any emergencies that might arise. The emphasis was on "no-decompression" diving, excursions where a direct ascent to the surface was always a viable avenue of escape if something went wrong. The training and skills were therefore built around that premise.

The result of these changes was a boom in the diving industry. From once being a sport that only the young, brave and super-fit could enjoy, now virtually everyone could learn to dive.

However, having started swinging, the pendulum of change kept moving, as pendulums are designed to do. Over time, not only did diver training become less physically and mentally challenging, the trend towards shorter and cheaper courses meant that divers were being certified with less-developed skills and very little diving experience. Importantly, beginner diver courses began to incorporate very little stress at all and less importance was accorded to crucial skills such as mask-clearing, which require that students exert a degree of mental discipline and which, in many cases, take time for an instructor to teach properly: time that, in present-day course structures, an instructor just does not have.

Additionally, with the pendulum now having swung almost 180 degrees from the days when instructors boasted about students who could not survive their courses, today it is very rare for a diver to fail. It would be nice to think that this is the case because instructors continue to work with their less able students until they acquire the necessary skills. In practice, though, with time constraints and the universal expectation on the part of both students and the industry that nobody will fail, the truth is that many divers are certified despite the fact that they cannot perform basic self-rescue skills and, therefore, when they dive, are always just one minor equipment malfunction away from a panicked bolt to the surface. I discuss this further in the chapter "Masking the Problem."

Technical Diver Training

Over the same period that initial sport diver training was becoming less challenging, opportunities were growing at the far end of the difficulty spectrum for sport divers to engage in extended decompression dives with new gasses and types of equipment in real and virtual overhead environments. This trend was dubbed technical diving and it required levels of skill and training far beyond those that sport divers were used to.

Because of this, the confined water skills sessions in technical diver training initially seemed unnecessarily sadistic to uninformed outsiders, and "beasting" and other epithets used in the early days of scuba started to surface again. There is a huge difference, however, between attitudes in those days and the concept behind the way technical diver training is run today.

Technical diving courses are tough because the risks involved in technical diving are greater than in mainstream sport diving. Technical diving demands dedication of time and effort.

Courses are academically challenging; there is a vast quantity of information to digest and a huge amount of maths. They are also physically challenging with many hours of skills sessions and several long dives, during which students are confronted with a number of staged life-threatening incidents to deal with.

Complacency is a major threat to the safety of a technical diver. People who sign up for the courses often have a great deal of diving behind them and think that they already know everything. The initial confined water skills session is designed to be a sharp reality check, a reminder to the students that, despite their experience, at these levels they are just beginners. I referred in the chapter "The Road from Instructor to Scuba Professional" to an instructor trainer who panicked during a technical pool session. The concept of pushing the students to a point where they may break helps both you and them identify any weaknesses in skills, mind-set, attitude or teamwork that need to be strengthened if they are to become safe technical divers.

This training concept requires the instructor to devise artificial situations mimicking real life emergencies that will induce stress in the students. The students are faced with problems to solve, and their failure provides the instructor with opportunities to make teaching points in circumstances where the student is in the perfect state of mind to receive them. When divers make mistakes, particularly mistakes that they knows could threaten their survival if the mistakes were made in a real life situation, then the memory will become seared permanently into the their minds. These experiences will also dispel complacency and encourage the diver to continue to practice and maintain the crucial skills and instincts acquired in training beyond the course so that they do not get forgotten.

Divers learn the skills and techniques required to survive emergencies and repeat these until their performance becomes automatic. This creates a physical memory of a series of procedures that the divers will deploy instinctively, should similar emergencies occur for real in the future. Also, the knowledge that they have encountered the problem many times before in training and dealt with it successfully gives them confidence and this is another crucial weapon in their survival armoury.

A significant challenge for instructors running technical diver training is that they have to control divers who may be on the verge of panic and keep them from harm, which is why the initial skills sessions always take place with a small number of students and in a shallow confined water location.

It is not just a question of skills: there are other things that set recreational diving and technical diving apart. To end, here are two examples of the sort of mind-set common among experienced mainstream sport divers that is a survival threat in a technical diver.

Example 1: Luis the Lone Wolf

Luis was a very experienced instructor. He signed up for a technical diving course and was determined to show me his stuff. Noticing this in the confined water session where he performed very well, I made him team leader for the first dive of the course.

Arriving at depth, he gave an OK signal, indicated the direction of travel and then started swimming along the wall. For someone wearing doubles and a stage cylinder for the first time, his buoyancy and trim were excellent. He had a powerful fin stroke and looked good in the water. The only problem was that his team were not faring so well and they quickly fell behind.

It is crucial that a dive team swim together, stay in visual contact and not drift too far apart. This is so that they can always use their combined forces and gas supply to help a team member who gets into difficulty. On training dives, if I see that any members of a team do not have this basic requirement at the forefront of their minds, a tactic I deploy is to initiate a simulated out of air emergency, where I signal to one diver that they have experienced a sudden catastrophic air loss and need to share air with one of their teammates. Once they have made contact and established stable air sharing I end the drill and the dive continues, with the team a little more aware of the need to stay close together and be aware of each other's status.

On this particular dive, therefore, with the team leader swimming off into the distance, I created a number of simulated team emergencies, all of which the divers had to handle without Luis their leader and which caused them to fall still further behind. Half way through the planned bottom time, Luis reached the planned turn point of the dive. He waited patiently for the others to catch up, flashed a quick OK sign, indicated that the team should turn around and headed off again. He arrived at the ascent point right on time; the others in his team, who had fallen behind again, were late. This meant extended decompression time during which one of the divers had to go to the hang tank for decompression gas to finish the final stop.

With everyone back on the boat, equipment stowed and drinks in hand, we all went to the bow for the dive debriefing. Luis smiled at me, evidently expecting to be praised for his excellent skills and technique. Instead, I said nothing and handed the debrief over to the dive team, asking them for their opinion of their leader's performance. They completely savaged him. All the resentment, frustration and anger built up during the ninety-minute dive spilled out and I just let the debate ensue. The lessons Luis was learning from his teammates were being transmitted with much more force and passion than I could ever muster and it is likely that he still remembers that session to this day. I do, and I was just the observer.

Luis had run the dive as if it was a competition where the participants were given points for individual merit rather than a team exercise where, unless everyone succeeds, they all fail. In mainstream sport diving, despite the much-touted but largely ignored buddy system, a diver functions alone and only looks for others when an emergency strikes. In technical diving, the team is always stronger than the sum of its parts and much of the training is designed to reinforce this concept. The reason why students often fail the stress tests in the early phases of confined water training is that they try to solve the problems alone. Once they start working as a team, solutions are much easier to find.

Example 2: Getting Priorities Mixed Up

Alex was a student on a cave diver training course. He was given the task of recovering the reel and line he and his team had initially used to connect a point outside the cave with the beginning of the permanent line in the cave, which in this case lay at a depth of around 30m (100ft.) He took the reel off the line and, as he started winding it up, he jammed it. He stopped to unjam the reel and was fiddling with it unsuccessfully when his instructor swam over, grabbed the reel from his hands, quickly wound a few turns of line around the body of the reel instead of the spool and thrust it back with a clear signal that Alex should get on with his ascent and forget about the (expletive deleted) reel.

Alex had made the sort of mistake very common among trainee technical divers; that of getting his priorities mixed up. He had been worrying about keeping the reel looking pretty rather than his increasing decompression burden, which was the one thing that should have been at the forefront of his mind.

The simultaneous introduction of multiple stress factors in technical diver training is designed to get the diver thinking straight, which is not always easy at depth where narcosis plays a factor and interferes with intellectual processes. Therefore divers have to know instinctively that, for instance, if a regulator starts to free flow while they are in mid water raising a submersible marker buoy (SMB), the regulator problem has to be taken care of immediately even if it means letting go of the SMB. This is one good reason why all technical divers should carry two SMBs!

Be professional by

Understanding the methods behind the apparent madness of technical diver training.

11. Masking the Problem

There are many divers who harbour a dangerous secret. Hermione is one of them. On a recent dive, the latest of over 200 she has done over the past 12 years, the unthinkable happened. Despite having followed her usual careful pre-dive cleaning routine, half way through the dive her mask started fogging up. The dive guide was pointing out small creature after small creature and eventually the fog became so thick she could not see what he was showing her.

She screamed into her mouthpiece in frustration and the dive guide, looking at her, indicated that she should clear her mask. She dimly perceived his signals through the mist and squealed again, signalling with her thumb that she wanted to go up. They ascended and when they arrived at the surface, Hermione made herself positively buoyant, took off her mask, flushed it out, spat in it, wiped the spit around and flushed it out again before replacing it on her face carefully and brushing strands of hair out from beneath the rim.

The divemaster waited patiently and when she had finished he asked why they had had to ascend and why she had not just cleared her mask underwater. "Because I CAN'T!" she screeched, still stressed. " I never could."

Hermione's secret, one shared by more divers than you would imagine, is that she lives every dive terrified of getting water into her mask and on to her face. So she is certainly not going to voluntarily allow water to enter her mask so she can defog it. She knows that if she does this or if her mask ever fails in any way, there is a good chance that she will panic and bolt to the surface. She therefore spends every dive conscious that she is always potentially seconds away from disaster.

Yet she is so keen on the sport that she continues to dive nevertheless, hoping that it will never happen. Over time, this hope turns into a misplaced conviction. The false logic she applies is that if she has done x hundred dives and has never had a mask leak, been caught by a flying fin or had a mask strap break, then none of these things will happen on the next x hundred dives either. And, if her mask fogs up then she can always ascend and sort it out on the surface, even though this may spoil the dive.

Teaching Troubles

It does not feel natural for anyone to have water covering their nostrils while they are breathing through their mouth. A lot of people understandably become anxious in such circumstances, worrying that they may inadvertently inhale water and choke. However, it is a common experience for divers to be underwater with water inside their mask and we teach them in their beginners' course how to manage their anxiety and deal with this as well as how to deal with an emergency situation where they lose their mask completely and have either to replace it or ascend without it. Nevertheless, as we see from Hermione's example, evidently there are divers who become divers without actually learning to manage the skills or their anxiety.

How can we as professionals manage this problem? We can try to tackle it at the source. Agencies can train instructors better, greater focus can be placed on mask skills in beginners' training and instructors can be told to insist on mastery of mask skills as a pre-requisite of graduation.

However, some people need more time to learn than others, especially when the things they have to learn involve overcoming fears that can be deep-seated. Today, with large classes and tight schedules there is often little time for extra lessons or one-on-one sessions and both students and dive centre bosses expect a 100% pass rate on courses. So the Hermiones of the future will continue to slip through the system. In the chapter "Real Risk Awareness" I tell the story of another diver who slipped through and how it happened.

When divers embark on technical diver training, they are put through a rigorous stress-testing session in confined water. This gives them experience of difficult situations and teaches them how to resolve these situations. The training also guides them towards adopting a mind-set where they work to build instinctive reactions, which replace fear and stress as the automatic response to difficult situations. A large part of these sessions is run with the diver not wearing a mask and technical instructors find that although the students may have had no difficulty performing the mask skills when they first learned to dive, nevertheless they still find it hard to stay calm and think logically when they have no mask on. However, when they are given multiple tasks to do underwater with no mask on, their focus shifts to the job in hand and gradually their fears fall away completely. Breathing underwater without their nose and eyes covered becomes completely natural and this does wonders for their confidence.

A Clinical Solution

So how do we get Hermione and others like her to this level without requiring them to sign up for technical diver courses? The solution is mask clinics. Many sports encourage their adherents to keep in shape and improve their performance by attending regular training sessions and scuba diving should be no exception. Indeed dive clubs and dive centres often run pool sessions during the off seasons to keep divers involved and give them opportunities to practice their skills. Some of these sessions could be designated as mask clinics.

The mask clinics would be open to all divers. Technical divers could practice stress tests; divers of less exalted rank could practice mask clearing or replacing a mask and more advanced divers could work on achieving technical-diver-esque levels of no-mask confidence.

Attending only one such clinic would not solve Hermione's issues at a stroke but perhaps she could start off by spending the first session just snorkelling up and down on the surface without a mask before moving on to scuba in a subsequent session. With divers of all experience levels there, no stigma would be attached to attending the clinics and therefore Hermione need not be embarrassed by her problem.

As the instructors running the clinics would be operating outside of a formal course structure, they would not be restricted to standard training agency teaching techniques and could develop no mask games or competitions to help build diver confidence and make the sessions more fun.

Eventually Hermione would conquer her fears and finally be able to enjoy her diving without the constant fear of impending doom looming at the edge of her consciousness.

Be professional by

Recognising that many divers have long-term problems with mask skills and that these represent a significant safety issue. Doing something about it.

12. School's Out!

Bali's Nusa Penida is the venue for quite a few of the tales told in Scuba Professional. There are a number of reasons for this. First Nusa Penida is an area I know well. Second, it is a challenging place to scuba dive and the cool, deep, fast moving water can catch divers out if they are not well prepared. Therefore many incidents take place there and the incidents raise useful points for discussion. Finally, I have many friends who lead trips out to Nusa Penida, so I hear a lot of the stories first-hand.

An Instructors Fun Dive

The group of four guys who star in this chapter are all instructors and trained technical divers. One day last year they decided to go out on a dive to look for manta rays and mola-mola, the oceanic sunfish that Nusa Penida is famous for attracting at certain times of the year. It would just be the four of them: no new divers or guests around to distract them or spoil the fun. They were aware that the search for the mola-

mola could take them into deep water, so they were all equipped with back-mounted double cylinders or twin side-mounted independent single cylinders. A couple of them had just completed a side mount course in open water and were practicing with this new configuration. Their back gas was air and they also had decompression cylinders on the boat filled with NITROX 40.

As they were gearing up on the boat, one of the divers clipped on a decompression cylinder but the other three decided against carrying an extra cylinder on the basis that it would just over-burden them.

It was an eventful dive. They descended on to a shallow cleaning station and immediately found a group of manta rays sweeping in to get serviced. However, the ocean swell crashing against nearby cliffs and then rebounding made it difficult for the divers to maintain their position in the water. They often had to swim hard against the surge to keep the mantas in view.

Once they had seen enough manta action they headed into deeper water away from the cliffs in search of a thermocline and, they hoped, some mola-mola hiding in the cooler water below. At around 36m(120ft.) they found exactly what they were looking for. A blurry shimmer in the sea announced the presence of a cool upwelling, carrying temperatures of 19C(66F.) Two enormous sunfish were lurking within, the parasites on their large disc-shaped bodies being picked off by a school of black, yellow and white bannerfish.

The divers were understandably excited and stayed watching and photographing the sunfish for several minutes. Looking at their computers they knew they had gone into decompression but they were quite relaxed about this, despite the fact that none of them had actually planned the dive. After all, they all had at least two cylinders. They could think about taking care of whatever decompression burden they had accrued when they eventually got back to the shallows. Unfortunately, none of the divers was monitoring their air supply closely so nobody realised that the combination of the surge, the depth, the cold water and the thrill of seeing all the big fish had caused their breathing rate to rise to a higher level than usual.

The Fun Turns Serious

It was the diver with the decompression cylinder who noticed first. He glanced at the gauges on his side-mounted twins and saw to his surprise that he had only 40bar (600psi) and 60bar (900psi) remaining. He signalled to the others that he was ascending and started to move up beyond the thermocline and back towards the shallows. After a few minutes he felt a tug on his arm and turned to find one of his buddies showing him that the pressure gauge on his doubles was reading 20bar (300psi.) After a few minutes of confusion, during which they used up even more of their rapidly diminishing breathing supply, the diver who had the most air unclipped his decompression cylinder and passed it to the other diver. They then both headed up to start their decompression stops which by then totalled over 30 minutes.

With all the water movement in the shallows they drifted apart and became separated. The diver who now had the decompression cylinder had enough gas to complete his stops comfortably and eventually ascended alone and returned to the boat. The other diver, who had relinquished the decompression cylinder, now realised that, without it, he no longer had enough gas to complete his own decompression. He looked up and the sight of the other two divers coming towards him raised his hopes. However, they were swiftly dashed when he saw what their gauges were showing. They were in exactly the same predicament as he was.

With air supplies down to almost zero and no sign of the diver with the decompression cylinder, the three divers realised that their best option was for one of them to go to the surface, omitting his remaining decompression stops, swim to the boat, get a couple of full cylinders with regulators attached and come back down with them. The diver with the least amount of decompression time remaining bravely volunteered and did exactly that.

Luckily, all the divers survived unharmed. The diver who had blown his stops and redescended spent the journey back to the dock breathing emergency oxygen as a precaution but he felt no symptoms of decompression illness. Nobody spoke much on the return journey; it had been a chastening experience.

While the Cat's Away

There is a popular maxim that says, "While the cat's away, the mice will play." There they were, all good divers who knew what they were doing, on a fun dive looking for big fish. There was nobody else around: no technical instructor to judge or reprimand them: no trainee divers who might follow their example. School was well and truly out! So why not just relax and let the rules slide for once? No need to worry about planning. They all had two cylinders and lots of air. If they ran into a bit of deco, they would just do the stops. What could go wrong?

Telling the story later, they described this as a technical dive. This was not a technical dive. A technical dive has pre-set parameters and is planned in detail with potential risks assessed and prepared for. This was just a deep, long dive in difficult conditions approached casually and carelessly by a group of divers who should have known better and who could have ended up paying for their carelessness with their lives.

The certification cards they hold show that they were all trained in decompression diving procedures by good technical diving instructors and all had the skills to execute a deep, long dive successfully. They had all planned a number of complex technical dives in the past and knew how to calculate gas requirements, compute decompression plans and work as a team to ensure the safe return to the surface of all the divers in that team.

Instructional Issues

What they had apparently not been taught sufficiently well is that the rules and procedures for decompression diving apply to all decompression dives, not just dives when someone is looking over your shoulder or when you have students with you. It is possible also that they were not accustomed to taking responsibility for the planning when no technical instructor was around. Perhaps their instructors had taken too much of a hands-on role during their training and had not prepared them adequately for dives when no instructor was present?

When you are teaching a course at any level, you must make sure that the students realise that they are not being taught the skills and procedures just in order to pass the course. You are not asking them to dive in a certain way just to please you or in order to satisfy training agency requirements. You need to insist that what you are teaching them are new habits that need to be practiced beyond the training course, on every dive, no matter if you are there watching them or not.

A couple of the points I touched on in the chapter "It All Comes Down to Me" are relevant here. By the final dive in the course, you as the instructor should be in the role of passive observer. Of course you are still responsible for the successful completion of the dive but you should not be a necessary component. The students, as a team, should be able to demonstrate all the skills and knowledge required to complete a dive at the level being taught without your intervention or assistance. The reason for this is obvious; on the next dive they do at this level, you will not be there. So if they are dependent in any way on your presence in order to complete a successful dive, add more training dives because they are evidently not yet ready to go out on their own.

Leave your ego behind. Part of your job when teaching any course is to make yourself surplus to requirements by the end of the course. You have to give the students the skills, knowledge and self-confidence to complete the dives without you. Yes, it is always nice to be needed but a huge pleasure of teaching is to take under your wing a person who wants to achieve goals that they cannot reach without you and release them a few days later with all the competence and confidence to achieve the goals on their own.

This story also illustrates one of the most common mind-sets that lead to instructors and experienced divers coming to harm. They know the right way to dive; they preach the right way to others but at some point they start to believe that the rules no longer apply to them. Complacency kills. There are no occasions when the rules for safe diving can be ignored. This is a very important message that must be delivered by instructors at every level and delivered unambiguously.

Short Cuts and War Stories

The importance of avoiding ambiguity was highlighted by an episode that occurred in the UK a few years ago. A professional rebreather diver nearly died when he was overcome by hypercapnia caused by the failure of his unit's carbon dioxide (CO_2) scrubber. After he had recovered, an enquiry was conducted to find out what had gone wrong. It turned out that instead of following conventional procedures and replacing the sodium hydroxide in his CO_2 scrubber completely after several hours of use, he had taken to adopting measures designed to make the material last a little longer and save him a little money. Instead of throwing the used sodium hydroxide away, he would remove it, spread it out in the sun to dry and pick out and dispose of any big lumps. Then he would put the rest back in the canister, adding a little fresh sodium hydroxide to top it off.

Immediately identifying this as the issue that had caused the problem that had nearly killed the diver, the appalled, investigators asked him where he had come up with such a notion and he told them that it was something his instructor had mentioned during his rebreather course.

The instructor was summoned to explain and at first he denied having ever taught anyone to do such a stupid thing and insisted he always followed the correct procedures. Then it dawned on him. He remembered that one evening over drinks he had entertained his students with tales from his Navy days, when shortages of CO_2 absorbent material in remote locations had meant that they had been forced to resort to extreme measures to extend the material they had. Evidently, one of the students had been so impressed by the story that he had adopted the procedure not in an emergency but in a foolish attempt to reduce his expenses!

Unfortunately, it is in the nature of humans to seek easier ways to do things. There will always be students who try to come up with bright ideas to get around the more irritating or time-consuming practices and procedures that you have taught them, even though you may have warned them of the dangers of taking short cuts. The worst thing you can do as an instructor is actually give them some of these bright ideas yourself. Avoid the temptation to impress your students with "war stories," even when you are speaking outside class and off the record. You are always on stage when you are teaching. You have to stay firmly on message all the time.

Be professional by

Building student habits.
Insisting on consistency.
Removing student dependency.
Watching what you say, even when you are "off duty."

13. The Value of Assistants

The other day I watched a dive instructor take two students out on a night dive. He prepared the gear, packed the truck, picked the students up from their hotel then unpacked everything at the beach, supervised the students as they set up their equipment then briefed them on the dive. Everyone put their gear on and he tidied up the dressing area before leading them into the water. After the dive, the instructor again took care of everything, including handing out drinks and snacks and driving the students back to the hotel.

The instructor was working hard, rushing about everywhere and his students obviously had a great time but it made me think; "why doesn't he have anyone to help him?"

What If?

Both students and instructor would have benefitted enormously from having someone else from the dive centre around on the beach, in the water or both.

The instructor would have had much less stress and fewer distractions before the dive so he could have focussed more on the students and the actual teaching. During the dive, he would not have had nagging on his mind the safety of the pile of expensive equipment he had left on the beach unattended. And after the dive, he could have left the logistics to an assistant while he debriefed the students.

With my technical diving "What If?" hat on, I thought about the safety issues too.

Without an assistant, what if the instructor had become incapacitated during the dive, either through sudden illness or a marine life sting? How would the two new divers have rescued him, removed him from the water, administered oxygen and and/or First Aid and summoned assistance?

Without an assistant, what if a current had picked up or weather set in, making it impossible for the instructor and students to return to their starting point?

Without an assistant, what if one or more students had encountered a problem early on and had been forced to abort their dive?

A Little Help

Of course, the last point in particular is something that instructors working alone and teaching classes with multiple students have to deal with all the time. If a student has a "dive-ending" problem during a class, be it failure to equalise on descent, an involuntary rapid ascent, an equipment problem or something else, the instructor has three alternatives. One: abandon the student with the problem and stay with the majority of the class. Two: take care of the student with the problem and abandon the others. Or three: assemble the whole group and abort the dive.

Of course, option 3 is the one that any right-thinking instructor would take but it is far from a satisfactory option as it involves wasting the time of those on the dive who did not have a problem but have paid for the instructor's time.

If the instructor has a little help at hand, either at the surface, under water or ideally both, then his options are much wider and considerably more attractive.

Common Sense

In the United Kingdom, there is legislation governing recreational scuba diving instruction and any circumstances where a diver is "at work." For every open water dive in open water, (that is, not confined water,) there must be a minimum of three supervisors, the instructor, at least one assistant in the water and at least one assistant on the boat or on shore, (for a beach dive.)

An assistant in the water, who must be qualified in diver rescue, gives the instructor a second pair of eyes and looks after the other divers if the instructor's attention is diverted by the need to take care of one particular student. The in-water assistant is also there to step in and deal with the emergency if the instructor gets into difficulty during the dive: hence the requirement for diver rescue qualification.

Assistants on the boat or on shore can help the instructor in a whole host of ways, such as assisting in operational logistics, but their primary job is to arrange and supervise the removal of a unconscious casualty to a point of safety. It is unlikely that an instructor and an in-water assistant in full gear with a number of other divers to take care of would be able to do this without losing valuable time. As a minimum all boat / shore assistants should have First Aid and CPR qualifications and be trained in the use of the on-site oxygen administration equipment.

The United Kingdom legislation was brought in following a series of diving accidents that came to the notice of Health and Safety authorities. After investigating these incidents, the authorities concluded that existing scuba diving safety procedures were inadequate and that, left alone, the training agencies would not act on their own to create and enforce the sort of procedures that would prevent a recurrence of this spate of accidents. So they stepped in, created the necessary legislation and set up enforcement teams.

A Guide Only

Instructors are not the only ones who could use a little help from time to time. A guide on a dive boat in Malaysia, who always used to run the diving on his own, tells the story of the time he dropped in to check the current while his group were gearing up on the boat. While he was down, the boat drifted near some rocks and the driver fired up the engines to take them clear. The jolt caused one of the divers, who had been sitting precariously on the gunwale, to fall into the water and start drifting away.

The boat driver evidently decided to wait for the guide to ascend before going to recover the drifting diver. However, seeing that the boat was not coming, the diver, who was newly certified, concluded that the best thing to do was to descend and go and find the guide. Luckily, other, more experienced divers were on board and, quickly assessing the situation, they dropped into the water too and took care of the situation, bringing the first diver back to the surface and inflating a marker buoy.

When they got back to the dock, the guide insisted that the divers who had saved the day be given a refund of the cost of their dive day. That was the last time he ever ran a trip without an assistant on board!

Teamwork

Instructors and their assistants must work together as a team and have specific roles assigned. They must know what their job is and be trained in how to do it.

I once saw an instructor lining up sets of equipment on the beach for a couple of customers doing a scuba experience. He opened all the cylinder valves then turned each valve handle back half a turn before moving away to brief the divers. A few minutes later, while his back was turned, his van driver arrived on the scene and, evidently eager to help, he went along the row of cylinders again, closing the cylinder valves, then turning them back on half a turn.

I attracted the instructor's attention and told him what had happened. At first he didn't believe me but when he checked the status of the valves he went white at the realisation of what could have happened if the divers had taken these cylinders into the water with the valves only partially open.

Why Leave Instructors Helpless?

Why are many dive operations reluctant to provide instructors with trained personnel to help them when they teach?

It is obvious that if dive operations are under-staffed, this can lead to all sorts of problems. Throughout Scuba Professional I describe difficult situations that could have been prevented and avoided simply by assigning more staff to the job. Not only can divers come to harm, but diving accidents can be very costly to dive centres, both economically and in terms of the damage that can be done to their reputation.

Why do instructors themselves not insist on assistants? Are they too proud to ask for help? Are the commissions they earn for courses too small for them to share with an assistant or two? Or do they believe their own propaganda and think that their superhuman skills extend to being able to do the job of several people simultaneously?

My best guess is that, in these days of cost-cutting competition, it is sometimes the case that safety issues are ignored in favour of economic considerations. If fewer staff are employed for a task, then costs are lower. This allows the dive operation to set cheaper prices and attract cost-conscious shoppers who will buy, ignorant of the safety compromises that have made these cheap prices possible.

A Solution of Limited Value

A solution to under-staffing that some dive centres come up with is to use dive master candidates or trainee instructors as assistants. They offer a tempting source of highly motivated employees who are actually paying for the privilege of working. However, dive operations need to be fair and bear in mind that, having spent money in anticipation of acquiring valuable experience, these trainee supervisors must be given work that is commensurate with their expectations. They should not just be assigned the monotonous tasks that the full-time staff do not want to do, such as cylinder filling or rinsing wetsuits.

At the same time, they must not be assigned roles for which they are not qualified. In the chapter "Drift Diving Disasters," I tell the story of a trainee supervisor who was assigned to help run a type of dive of which she had no prior experience. It nearly ended in tragedy. In this case the dive centre was dishonest and falsely represented to the divers that there were two qualified staff looking after them, when, in fact, there was only one. The concept of using trainees has value but it is limited. They are not always a valid substitute for employing properly qualified and paid staff.

Be professional by

Recognising the value of assistants.

§3

Scuba Operations

14. Running Your Own Dive Business:
Lessons Learned

Generally speaking, two types of people set up new dive operations. The first type are keen divers who have made some money in a career that has nothing at all to do with scuba diving and decide that they will change their lives and combine work and play. The second type are long-term dive instructors who are fed up of working for others and want to strike out on their own, do things their way and organise their lives so that they are the ones who benefit from their hard work.

In the mid-1990s, both of these descriptions applied to me. I was working full time for the Hong Kong Government and also teaching diving professionally in the evenings and at weekends. On a whim, I decided to leave this life behind and set up my own dive centre. The location I chose was Guam, an island east of the Philippines in the Western Pacific that belongs to the USA and is the travel hub for the scattered islands of Micronesia that include famed dive destinations like Truk,

Palau, Yap and Bikini Atoll. They were great years but it was very hard work with long hours and no seasonal break.

Guam is a major travel destination for Asian scuba divers and it also has a large population of resident scuba divers, mostly US military servicemen and their families. So my operation was unusual in that it was both a resort dive centre that catered to tourists and an urban dive store for divers living on Guam. This allowed me to experience what it is like to run a dive operation in both "worlds."

In this chapter I run through a few things that I learned you have to do when you set up and run a dive business. Many of these probably apply to setting up and operating a business in any field: some may be unique to diving. I picked a number of the lessons up the hard way; by first making every mistake possible before chancing on the correct solution. Others, more by luck than good judgement, I managed to get right from the start.

Choose Your Market

The scuba diving market is wide and, right from the beginning, you have to decide where your focus will be, identify which group of divers you will mostly be dealing with and set the business up to cater to their specific needs. You cannot be all things to all people. You have to specialise. If you try to cover the whole spectrum, you will only achieve mediocrity. Specialising helps you build expertise, acquire a good industry reputation and develop a dedicated client base. It also means you will not have the crushing daily burden of competing for customers with generalist dive operations in your area, whose products and services are often so similar they can only compete on one thing, price.

So decide what you will specialise in and do it excellently. Choose a field that suits your environment and your skill set. Your specialisation might simply be divers from a particular city, country or language group. It might be interest-based: cave diving, free diving or macro-photography perhaps. Or you might want to be known as a training centre and build a name for running outstanding diver courses.

Sometimes, the decision will be made for you simply by virtue of your location. For example, if you set up a dive operation in Truk, most of the folk who contact you will be wreck divers. You will not get many requests for beginners' courses. A few years ago, when muck diving first became popular, one resort in Ambon, Indonesia found that almost every diver who visited wanted to dive on one particular site under a jetty, which had become famous for unusual marine life but which was an hour's drive and thirty minutes boat ride from the resort. They initially tried to persuade divers to try out the nearby reefs instead but to no avail. So what did they do? They decided that muck diving would be their unique selling point and moved the resort, setting it up on the other side of the island, right next to the site where everyone wanted to go. It was not an easy decision to make but it turned out to be the right one.

Decide on Your Role

Before you embark on any enterprise, give careful thought to the role you will play in the company. Many new dive operators are "alcoholics who bought a pub." That is to say, their main incentive in opening a dive centre is to do more diving. Unless you have bottomless reserves of cash, a dive operation has to be run as a business rather than a hobby, or the business will not last long and you will become penniless fast.

So, if you are setting up the business because you love diving and intend to spend as much time as possible doing it, then, as you will be underwater much of the time, you need to employ a professional manager to run the company. Choose your manager carefully, respect and trust their experience and give them authority as well as responsibility; authority even to countermand the whimsical notions and schemes you will come up with from time to time. You will also need a manager if you decide that your role in the dive operation is primarily to teach. You cannot be an effective instructor if you are not able to give your full attention to your students and you cannot do that if you have business issues constantly whirling around in your mind.

Of course, one of the main reasons people start their own businesses is so that they can be the boss. So if you are planning to run the operation yourself and employ others to do the teaching and diving, make sure you know what you are doing. If you do not already have management experience then sign up for some business courses to teach you how to look after both people and cash flow.

Find Your Own Customers

This is the hardest thing of all but probably the most important. You must develop your own customer base. You start building a customer base as soon as you begin teaching diving and the only way to do this effectively and ethically is by doing such a great job that divers remember you. People still stop me at dive shows asking after instructors and guides who worked for me in the Guam days and who left such an impression that the divers they taught or guided have vivid memories of them even decades later. If any of them started their own businesses, they would have a crowd of folk flocking to dive with them.

What you do NOT do, while you are working for a company that is not your own, is try to build a client base for the future by taking contact details from customer files and keeping in touch with them unilaterally in your own right rather than as a representative of the company. This is a major breach of professional ethics and probably a breach of your contract too.

When you have your own dive business, if you are the one who is attracting the customers then you are in control. If you depend on other entities such as hotels, travel companies or tour operators then your business is in the hands of people who do not have your interests as a major priority.

If your circumstances or business model depend on acquiring business from agents, think very carefully about how much you charge and how the payment arrangements may affect your cash flow. Normally, an agent will take the money from the customer in advance and will only pay you a long time, sometimes several months, after the service has been provided. The agent will also take a significant percentage. If you object to the terms, the agent will find another provider, unless of course your service is unique or you have a strong reputation, (see my points above concerning the need to specialise,) in which case you have a powerful negotiating tool, as the customers want you and the agent has little influence on their purchasing decision.

If your business is linked with a hotel or several hotels, first, you are dependent for your customers on the hotels' ability to attract guests. Second, you may have a business connection with the hotel or you may even be located in the grounds of the hotel but this does not necessarily guarantee that hotel staff will actively sell your services, or that hotel guests who want to dive will choose you.

To be secure, you have to recruit your own customers and, as I said, the best way of doing that it is to provide a first class service that divers will enjoy so much that they return frequently and recommend you to others. That's it; that's the secret. There is no short cut. You can do all the Tripadvisor tweaking you like; you can be a social networking whizz but running a great dive operation that always puts the interests of the customers first is the sole guaranteed recipe for success.

Choose Your First Staff Carefully

As a new dive business in town, it is highly likely that the first people who apply for any job you advertise will not be the cream of the crop, no matter how highly they talk themselves up. Beware of prospective staff members who go out of their way to disparage other dive businesses in your area. When I opened in Guam, I took on an instructor who had great qualifications but could not provide references because the people he was working with and for "were idiots and did not appreciate him." I completely failed to spot the warning signs.

Having completed the final day of work with his previous employer, he turned up at my dive centre with his gear in the back of a pick up. He parked the truck behind the shop, unloaded his bags, took a hose and some soap and started painstakingly washing each item of his equipment. I walked over, noticed a distinctive smell in the air and asked him what had happened. He revealed that, while he was in the office picking up his paperwork, his former colleagues had all gathered on the dock, opened his dive-bags and collectively urinated on them and in them, as a parting gift. Now I heard the alarm bells! But it was too late; I was already committed to a contract. Luckily there was a trial period specified. He did not last long. Unless you are well acquainted with the local community, be wary. Avoid entering into any long-term commitments. Perhaps take staff on in a part-time role first.

When I subsequently went on to take over a diver-training agency in the United Kingdom, I encountered a similar phenomenon. As in Guam, I was the new guy and did not know many of the personalities I was dealing with. Several disaffected instructors from rival training agencies applied to join up as soon as I took over, saying they were unhappy with their current situation. Suspicious, I took the then-unprecedented step of contacting the heads of my principal rival agencies and suggested meetings to compare notes on instructors who wanted to switch allegiance. The meetings generated close working relationships between the rival agencies that lasted many years and proved very useful, enabling us to deal easily with individuals who sought to set us against one another. Nobody ever imagined that we could actually work together.

Know Where Your Real Competition Lies

This success made me regret not having tried to develop similar links with rival dive operations when I first set up shop in Guam. As I described earlier, among other things, I could have used some help in filtering good job applicants from bad. At the time, I thought that any suggestion of mutual assistance would be rejected out of hand as competition was fierce and relations between dive centre owners often bordered on hatred. This is frequently the case all over the world wherever there is more than one dive centre in a town or on a beach.

However, I came to realise over the years that, as a scuba diving operation, your main competition does not come from within the sport. You lose far more customers to other pastimes and sports. In Guam, where the resident diving market was predominantly young, male and military, my main competitors for their leisure time dollars were strip clubs and golf courses, not other dive centres. In other parts of the world, the competition might be home improvement centres and Sunday morning football.

So make the effort to get to know the people who own and run other dive operations in your area. Be generous with your time try to build good relations. Never say anything derogatory about them in public and ignore anyone who would seek to create division between you by telling tales.

Don't Expand Too Quickly

Be wary too of taking on too many full time staff. Every dive business, every business that caters to tourists, is susceptible to seasonal booms and busts. In the boom times, it always feels like you need more staff but when times are quieter, a heavy payroll can quickly put you in financial difficulties. Yes, you can always find work for idle hands: painting, cleaning, fixing and tidying are important jobs, but none of them directly generate revenue.

You might think the answer is to employ freelance instructors and guides because you only have to pay them when you are busy. However, the chances are that during high season when you have a lot of customers so does every other dive operation, so part-time staff are hard to find.

A solution that worked for me, and works for many other dive operations, is one that I mentioned in the chapter "The Value of Assistants." You can develop professional training programmes and supplement your full time staff with divemaster and instructor interns. We are fortunate to work in an industry that people will pay to be part of. It is important, though, to respect the interns as you would any other professional, make sure that they get full value from the experience they are paying for and refrain from abusing them by just giving them the boring jobs or over-stretch them with tasks they are not qualified to do. Happy, satisfied interns recommend other interns and keep the flow going.

Employ an Accountant Early

Unless you are an accountant, find one before you open your doors, listen to them and take their advice. Do not use an accountant who is a diver as this person may not be able to view your business objectively. It is fascinating and sobering to get a glimpse of your dive business through the eyes of someone for whom diving has no romance. During the time I ran the diver training agency, I was asked by an accountant to describe my business. I explained how we taught dive instructors how to teach people to become good, safe divers using the materials we had developed and went on to describe how our trainees then went on to explore cave systems, discover historical shipwrecks and perform ultra deep excursions beyond the range of most scuba divers. He listened carefully to all this then concluded in a completely matter-of-fact way; "so you are a bookseller then."

Adhere to Maintenance Schedules

I referred in an earlier chapter to my good fortune in hiring an employee who was a former aircraft mechanic. Not only was Chuck a first class divemaster, boat captain and engineer, he also taught me a valuable lesson: run your dive operation around your maintenance schedules rather than the other way round. When he came on board, I asked him to set up schedules for the compressor, the mixing panel, the vehicles and all our diving equipment. He did this but made me promise that the schedules would always come first, ahead of diving plans and any other operational requirements. I agreed but, of course, the first time Chuck came in and reminded me that the compressor would be out of action the following day because a service was due, I tried to postpone it because we had a lot of divers in. He reminded me of my promise, I apologised and we made sure we had enough cylinders ready to take us through the down day. In six years, we never had a compressor problem; we never had a vehicle break down and we never had any house regulator or BCD malfunctions. That was all because we had maintenance schedules and we stuck to them.

Know how to Balance Success and Safety

When you work out the pricing for the services you offer, whether these are courses, dive trips, maintenance or equipment sales, avoid just picking prices similar to those offered elsewhere. Instead, calculate all the costs involved in supplying the product or service, decide on the profit margin you want to take and set the price accordingly. For courses and dive trips, remember to factor in agent commissions, staff time, fuel, equipment and vehicle depreciation – everything.

I do not think anyone deliberately sets out in business intending to cut corners or provide poor quality service. However, it is easy when you start out to set prices without factoring in all the costs. When you subsequently realise your mistake, you have three options, A, raise prices, B, lose money or C, cut corners. You may worry that raising prices will cause you to lose customers; you certainly do not want to lose money so there is a huge temptation to go for option C. This is a temptation that many cannot resist. In scuba diving, cutting corners usually involves reducing the number of staff you assign to a course or dive trip and this has significant safety implications. Elsewhere in Scuba Professional and especially in the chapter "The Value of Assistants" I discuss the problem of inadequate staffing in more detail.

The right answer to the dilemma is of course, option A. If you cannot get people to sign up for a course or dive trip at the price you need to charge to run it properly with ALL the safety boxes ticked and still make a little profit on top so you can stay in business, then you need to find another line of work.

If you are unlucky you might find yourself in a cut-throat environment where competitors will deliberately set prices so low that they lose money in an attempt to run off the opposition by encouraging them to follow them down the slippery slope. This is just a game of chicken where the person with the deepest pockets blinks last and wins and the competition is often motivated by emotion and personality conflict rather than business strategy. The best tactics to use if you see this happening are to remain aloof, stick to your guns, continue to do what you do well and rely on quality winning out. It takes nerve but your business survival depends on it.

Whatever you do regarding pricing, do not follow the example of JT, a friend of mine who, in the early days of NITROX, decided that he would set up in business to supply NITROX to all the dive operations in his area, so they did not have to invest in production equipment themselves. He showed me around his impressive facility and explained his business model to me. I asked him how much he charged for a cylinder of NITROX and he told me. The price seemed low. I made a swift back-of-the-envelope calculation and told him I thought he was losing money on every cylinder of NITROX he sold. "I know," he said, "I'm counting on the volume to make it work!" I had to explain to him gently that the more NITROX he sold, the more he would lose. He was dumbstruck!

Don't Ignore Half the World

Five incontrovertible facts: most diving equipment is made for men: men and women are not the same shape: many divers are female: there is no such thing as a unisex wetsuit: and finally, divers are much more likely to keep diving if they feel comfortable in their equipment.

In your fleet of rental equipment, you must have a range of wetsuits designed for ladies. Note the word "designed." I am not talking about buying a selection of men's wetsuits in pink and other pastel shades. If someone, male or female, young or old, comes to dive with you and rents a suit that does not fit, apologise profusely, do your best to fix the problem, perhaps by adding a rash guard, neoprene vest or skin suit underneath, and buy additional suits to make sure it never happens again. If you give a lady diver a wetsuit that fits her perfectly, there is a good chance that you will be the first dive centre ever to do this. Looking for a "WOW" factor? There you go!

Before choosing a range of rental BCDs, ask a few ladies of different shapes and sizes to try some on. You may be surprised to learn that one of the most successful designs for ladies is a soft pack harness with a small back-mounted wing. This is the same style of BCD that technical divers use. One problem that I had in Guam was that many of my divers were Asian ladies and I could not easily find BCDs that were not too large for them. The ideal solution I came up with was to buy BCDs from a small manufacturer in the USA that made dive equipment for teenagers.

Keep the Trash Can Empty

Finally, the best indicator that a dive operation is not well run is an overflowing trashcan. Some folk will walk into a place, take one look at a bin that has not been emptied for while and walk straight out again. "Hmm," they think, "if they cannot keep on top of the trash situation, what are the chances that they change their compressor filters on schedule, maintain their regulators properly or can be relied upon to look after me well on a scuba dive?"

Be professional by

Choosing your market.
Deciding on your role.
Finding your own customers.
Choosing your first staff carefully.
Knowing where your true competition lies.
Not expanding too quickly.
Employing an accountant early.
Abiding by maintenance schedules.
Knowing how to balance success and safety.
Not ignoring half the world.
Keeping the trash can empty.

15. Dive Briefings: Tell Me About It

Your mission, should you choose to accept it: take a group of divers with vastly different diving backgrounds, most of whom have never met before, and turn them into a united, disciplined team that will stay together and follow you obediently through a 60 minute dive.

Do you think you can do that? Great, you have five minutes to tell them exactly what you would like them to do in a way that will persuade them to do it. Then repeat the exercise at least twice a day with a different group of divers every day.

This is the life of a resort dive guide and it can be a tough mission.

With new divers, the task is usually straightforward because they have been conditioned by their recent training. Some are still dependent divers and think they need to stay close so that you can save them if something goes wrong. Others just stick with you because you told them to and you are the authority figure.

If you are guiding more experienced divers, however, your dive briefing is the crucial factor. In the five minutes available, you have to convince them that it is in their interests to stick with you as a group. If you do not give them sufficient valid reasons to do this, they will conclude that they do not need you and scatter all over the ocean, doing their own thing. Of course, they have every right to do this: they are certified and capable divers.

But staying in a group benefits everyone. It is good for you as a guide because it enables you to give your time and attention equally to all your customers. It also helps you keep to your timetable for the day and means you do not waste valuable time in an already tight schedule chasing over the ocean picking up stray divers at the end of the dive.

It is good for the customers from a safety point of view as both you and the other divers are always close at hand to assist in any emergency. Also, although some of the divers may actually have even more diving experience than you, they do not know your sites as well as you do. Here you are the expert, you know where everything is and you can take them on the perfect route that will enable them to get the most out of the site in the time available. By diving in a group with you, they will therefore have the optimum experience and get the best possible value for the money they are paying. This is great for the dive centre you work for too as it will encourage the divers to return as well as recommend the operation to others.

Briefing Techniques

The manner of your briefing depends on your personality but it is important that you take the opportunity to impose your authority. This does not mean that you should shout, scream and issue commands like a drill sergeant, although if that is your personality and it works for the people you take diving, go for it. Play whatever role you are comfortable with, as long as it is effective. Many dive guides just play nice and their divers follow them because they are likeable and they do not want to disappoint them. Others take on the role of benevolent cop, a little authority delivered with a smile, suggesting that the group had better do what they are told or there will be sharp words afterwards.

However, you cannot rely on your personality alone to keep your divers together in a group. In your briefing, it is crucial that you provide them with genuinely substantive grounds for doing the dive your way. These grounds might include the possibility of a strong current that would cause them to miss a mid-ocean pinnacle completely if they did not follow your lead. Or you might suggest that you know where certain hard-to-find and highly-prized creatures hang out and that the divers could miss them if they go it alone. Photographers will follow you to the ends of the earth if you can give them the prime shots they are looking for.

Dive Site Maps

Whenever possible use a map of the site to enable the divers to visualise where they will be going and what they will see. A map helps those who may decide to go on their own to plan their dive and ascend in the same general location as the main group. It also gives you an opportunity to point out identifiable physical features for the divers to use as waypoints. For instance, you could indicate a place where you would expect to be about halfway through the dive and where it would be a good idea to check how much air they have left.

Unless you are a gifted artist or draughtsperson and can conjure up works of art in a matter of minutes before every dive, then, for the sites you take people to frequently, create map boards and keep them on the boat. You have enough to do on a dive trip without having to draw a new site map before every dive. I once worked with an operation that had tee shirts decorated with line drawings of their popular sites, mostly shipwrecks. Before each dive, the guide would just pin the relevant tee shirt to the board and use that for the briefing. The dive centre sold a lot of tee shirts!

Although the map for the site may be the same every time, your briefing and dive plan will change according to the sea conditions and the composition of the group. So you need to be flexible. For instance, there may be a strong current running or visibility may not be as good as usual. If you have experienced divers with you the dive will be longer than if you have newer divers. Older divers will move more slowly than younger divers and you might have to choose a shorter route for them. If you have photographers in the group, then you may have to adjust the dive plan to accommodate their needs, or add more support staff to make sure they do not get detached from the group when they stop to take pictures.

So don't draw the route on your map boards in indelible ink. Mark it out while you are briefing. Use photographs as well. If you are planning to show the divers significant marine life that they may not have seen before such as a field of staghorn coral or a pair of ornate ghost pipefish, hand pictures around so they will know what they are looking at when you show them.

Debriefings

Divers may think they do not get debriefed after a dive but this is because it is usually a much less formal process than the briefing. It is not necessary to give fun divers the same sort of in depth performance assessment that you would deliver after a training dive. Instead, pass among your divers post-dive celebrating the cool sightings they have made, asking how they enjoyed the dive, remarking on a bubbling hose that needs replacing or the fact that one of the divers might be more comfortable if they removed a kilo from their weight belt. Monitor conversations among the group to spot possible personality conflicts or suggestions that a diver might have had a problem that you did not detect. This indirect feedback can also make you aware of things you may need to change when you run the dive for similar groups in future.

Boat Briefings

When divers go boat diving, the captain will normally deliver a general briefing before the boat sets off, although he can always delegate this to the guide. The briefing includes the layout of the vessel, safety procedures, emergency drills, company policy and diving logistics. Depending on whether the vessel is a day boat or liveaboard, it could take between 5 minutes and an hour. If it is going to be a long briefing, then make sure all the guests are in a warm, dry, place, free from distractions. Otherwise you will be just wasting your breath. An audience that is uncomfortable might be able to hear you but they are not listening and the boat briefing contains some important stuff.

A few years ago, I watched a live-aboard cruise director deliver a 45-minute boat briefing in the rain on a wet dive deck. He was in the dry under a tarpaulin; the divers were in wetsuits out in the open. On and on he went, seeming not to notice that the divers had started shivering, the wet neoprene wicking away their body heat in a reversal of the suits' underwater function. Finally, he finished and announced, "Let's go diving!" with both thumbs raised and a big toothy grin. However, his was the only smile on the dive deck. His charges just stared at him in total disbelief at the soul-numbing experience he had put them through.

He was not an inexperienced dive professional. It is possible that when he came out, he originally intended just to deliver a dive briefing, but it suddenly dawned on him that he had forgotten to deliver the boat briefing earlier. Realising this, he could have postponed it until after the dive or he could have changed the schedule, asked the divers apologetically to change back into dry clothes and brought them inside to listen to the boat briefing over a hot drink. They could then have gone back out and done the dive later. But, instead, he thoughtlessly ignored their comfort and well-being and, by doing so, succeeded in undermining himself right from day one and losing their support for the remainder of the trip.

When It All Goes Wrong

Sometimes, no matter how good your briefing is, your carefully constructed dive plan can fall apart as soon as you enter the water. Then you have to think on your feet and do your best to balance the safety of your divers with the need to show them a good time. This chapter concludes with a story that provides an excellent example of a dive that went wrong from the start but that ended with a moment of pure serendipity. Sometimes when you are a good dive professional, the ocean will reward you!

One morning Richard, an experienced instructor, took a group to a popular deep dive site where a crevice in the reef wall provided refuge for schooling fish. He checked with the boat captain that they had anchored in the right spot and then began his briefing. He told the divers that they would follow the anchor chain down to the reef top at around 15m (50ft,) where they should do a quick check of their equipment and air supply before they went deeper. Richard would then escort them over the reef wall and into the crevice, which bottomed out at 30m (100ft.) and which they could all explore at their leisure, keeping an eye on their no-decompression time remaining. He told them about the stands of scarlet sea whips that were a prominent feature of the site and suggested that photographers in the group might like to take photographs of their dive buddies hovering behind the whips, a classic image that has featured on countless diving magazine covers. He then mentioned a few other things they should see on the dive and talked them through the ascent plan.

The divers all got ready. Richard entered the water first, swam to the anchor chain and waited for the group to join him. When they were all assembled he gave the signal to descend and dropped down the line, looking up as he went down to make sure the divers were all following him. When he saw that they were, he turned his head and glanced down to get his bearings. However, instead of the reef wall, he could see nothing but deep, blue sea and the anchor chain disappearing off into the darkness below him.

The anchor had evidently pulled free while the divers were gearing up and nobody had noticed. Richard's comprehensive well-thought-out briefing was now completely redundant. The safety of his group in mid-water was his first concern and his first instinct was to abort the dive. Looking around, however, he concluded that all the divers in the group had sufficient experience to manage a blue water swim and he decided to lead them back to the reef where they might find something to see that would make the dive worthwhile. He thought they could not have drifted too far away from the wall.

By now, the group was all assembled around him at 21m (70ft) or so. Richard checked his compass to figure out where the wall should be and directed them all to follow him, indicating that they should maintain their current depth as they swam. It was ten minutes, (for Richard ten very long minutes,) before they finally saw the wall loom up ahead of them. They were already almost half way through the dive and so far they had seen absolutely nothing. Heading for the crevice was out of the question; it was too late to take the group deeper now. Richard would have to spend the rest of the dive on the reef top, desperately searching for things to entertain the divers and take their minds off the boring, blue water swim they had just done.

He was already dreading the looks and comments he would get when they got back on the boat. And then he saw the manta ray. Gliding effortlessly towards the divers, the huge winged beast slowed as it saw them and then rose in the water column and started circling and weaving, swooping and swirling around above them as if playing with the streams of bubbles they were creating. Cameras flashed and those without cameras just gazed on entranced. The manta was in no hurry to leave; it seemed just as entertained by the encounter as they were. Finally, with air supplies running low, it was the divers who had to take their leave. Back on board everyone was ecstatic: "What an incredible dive!" "Best dive of my life!" "Can't believe it just stayed and played with us!" The blue water swim and fact that they had not even seen the dive site they had been aiming at was not even mentioned.

Richard breathed a huge sigh of relief. He had dived along that reef wall dozens of times and had never seen a manta ray there before. He wondered if he should mention the possibility of a similar encounter when he took groups there in future but decided against it. Just as well: he never saw one there again.

Be professional by

Never underestimating the importance of good briefings.
Doing your best and trusting in the bounty of the ocean.

16. Where's the O2?

The dive boat had just arrived in Crystal Bay, a notorious diving accident black spot on the outlying Balinese island of Nusa Penida, when our attention was drawn by a burst of frenetic activity next to a neighbouring boat. A wet-suited figure was being manhandled over the side of the boat and laid out on deck. A couple of crewmen hunched over the figure while everyone else on board stood to one side, heads craned in concern. Seeing us approach, one of the crew shouted over and asked if we had oxygen. We did and we handed our big green DAN kit over to them as the boats met bow to bow. They turned and headed off at full speed to the nearest recompression chamber located on the main island of Bali a good 45 minutes rough ride away.

I never found out what happened to the injured diver nor what had caused the accident but the combination of cool water, fast current and depth at the edge of Crystal Bay has caused more than a few inexperienced divers to elect for a rapid ascent as a way of "just getting out of there!"

Once the key first aid concerns of monitoring consciousness, airway and breathing have been taken care of, the recommended treatment for suspected decompression illness (DCI) is administration of 100% oxygen. The oxygen should be delivered as soon as possible and continuously until there is no more oxygen available or until a diving doctor instructs that it should be interrupted. Therefore every responsible dive operation, whether boat or land-based, should carry a sufficient supply to allow a diver with suspected DCI to continue breathing oxygen until they arrive at a medical facility with oxygen on tap.

The diver in the above incident had unfortunately chosen to dive from a boat that was carrying no oxygen at all. Luckily for the crew and for the diver, (I hope,) we had happened by and were suitably equipped to help. Of course, this meant we no longer had oxygen and our dive operator had to deal with the dilemma of whether to continue with our dive plans for the day. But that is another story.

A Key Point

A key point you should cover in every dive briefing you give is "Where is the O2?" You should explain both where it is and who among the dive team that day is qualified to deliver it. There should be at least two of you. After all, what if the injured diver is also the oxygen delivery person?

It is not enough just to count on the presence of a big green box in the dive van or on the boat to reassure divers that you are prepared. Given that accidents that require immediate delivery of oxygen are thankfully rare, the oxygen kit in that green box can sit for a long time without being deployed. Stories abound in the dive industry of boat crews turning to the kit in an emergency and finding that the damaging marine environment has caused the rubber hoses to waste away and corroded the cylinder valve to the point of immobility!

So, when you are briefing the divers and telling them where the O2 is, don't just make a vague gesture in the direction of the big green box, make a point of opening it so the divers can see that the equipment is in good condition. Also be prepared to demonstrate that the cylinder is full if someone asks.

Every dive operator should have an established and rehearsed procedure regarding what action to take with an injured diver. I cover this in more detail in the next chapter "I Think I Might Be Bent." Sadly, many dive operations are both under-prepared and under-equipped to deal effectively with a diving emergency. In too many cases there is actually no plan to deal with an incident of decompression illness. The rationale often runs along the lines of "it hardly ever happens so it is not worth thinking about until it does."

Failing to Plan

Top dive operations are also sometimes guilty of failing to plan adequately. Even the best liveaboards will usually carry oxygen on board the mother-boat but not on the small tenders that ferry divers to and from the dive sites. Often this ferrying involves long rides to allow the mother-boat to float free in the deep channel away from the reefs. This means that if a diver blows to the surface, the nearest oxygen is a long way away and the delay in delivery could make the difference between tragedy and survival.

In some jurisdictions it is mandatory for dive boats and liveaboard skiffs both to have oxygen on board and at least a two-person crew. You may think this is just common sense and really should not have to be required by law. After all, it is almost impossible for an individual operating alone to bring an unconscious or disabled diver out of the water and into a boat. It is also impossible for one person to drive that boat and administer first aid and oxygen to an injured diver at the same time.

However outside those parts of the world where it is mandated by law, the practice of having oxygen and at least two people qualified to deliver it on board the closest boat to the divers is rarely followed. Even international companies that operate worldwide will only conform to these procedures in countries where the law requiring them is enforced. Elsewhere, they will ignore it completely. This is ample evidence that in scuba diving, as in many other fields of human activity, you can never rely on the fact that common sense and concerns over safety will over-ride considerations of economic gain, "business needs" or just pure idleness and neglect. That is why governments that want to keep their citizens from harm have to resort to legislation.

Be professional by

Always knowing where your O2 is.
Making sure your divers know this too.
Abiding by safety procedures because they are
common sense and save lives, not just because they are
required by local law.

17. I Think I Might Be Bent

This is something that will happen to you at some point in your career: maybe more than once. A diver in your charge will approach you after a dive or at the end of a dive day and say, "I think I might be bent." Your initial thoughts are likely to be negative.

"What?" You may think. "This is impossible. I was with this customer on every dive and there were no problems. I'm fine. No one else is complaining. They are just paranoid or looking for attention."

This type of reaction is understandable. It is awkward and time consuming for you to deal with a diver who has decompression illness (DCI.) There is also a stigma attached. Nobody wants to be the instructor or dive centre that "got someone bent."

Of course, this is illogical. No matter how well you plan and run dives, accidents can still take place, divers are human and make mistakes, physiological characteristics exist that predispose divers to DCI and nobody knows enough about DCI to be able to guarantee that it will not happen. Even now, dive computer algorithms and safe diving procedures are still just best guesses.

Nevertheless, it is sadly all too common for competing dive shops to accuse one another of unsafe practices and the fear of this can induce dive professionals to try to conceal accidents rather than deal with them.

So you might be tempted to try to persuade the diver that the symptoms they are feeling are just normal post dive twinges. Or you may invent another possible cause rather than DCI and suggest that the diver take an aspirin or two, go to bed early and see how they feel in the morning.

This is not what you do. Your status as a dive professional does not qualify you to make any type of diagnosis in situations like this. In every case of this sort, no matter how unlikely you privately think it is that the diver is really bent, you must let an expert decide how serious the situation is and advise you on what to do.

It is far, far better to act quickly and immediately following a set procedure (see below) than to delay your response and have a diver's symptoms worsen while you prevaricate. No one with any common sense will accuse you of acting incorrectly nor will you ever be accused of wasting anyone's time.

A Set Procedure

1. Ask the diver to lie down flat. This is most important if the diver is reporting symptoms soon after a dive.

2. Give the diver 100% oxygen to breathe as quickly as possible. This should be delivered via a medical oxygen

demand valve with a tight sealing mask. Failing that, use a non-rebreather mask with a reservoir but again make sure the seal is good so the diver is inhaling as high a percentage of O2 as possible.

3. Ask someone to monitor the diver, record the amount of time the diver breathes oxygen for and note any improvement or deterioration in the diver's symptoms.

4. Give the diver water to drink, (electrolyte type fluids are even better,) as long as they are fully conscious, their condition is not deteriorating quickly and they are not nauseous, vomiting or feeling stomach pain.

5. If they are conscious, ask the diver for details of: -

a. recent dives, particularly depths, times, deco stops, safety stops, rapid ascents and unusual events.

b. the diver's signs and symptoms, when they appeared and their severity and progression.

c. the diver's medical history including previous diving accidents, and

d. any medication the diver is taking

Make notes of what the diver says. Keep these notes as a permanent record.

6. Then call your DAN diving emergency hotline. Diving medical specialists staff these hotlines 24 hours a day, 7 days a week. You will always get through to someone.

(If the diver is unconscious, then of course go straight from point 3 to point 6.)

Key Points

You must call the hot line. It does not matter whether the diver is a DAN member or not and it does not matter whether the diver's symptoms ease or otherwise once they start breathing oxygen. Giving the diver oxygen is not a substitute for making the call. Nor should you wait until you have made the call and received expert advice before you put the diver on oxygen.

Keep the diver on 100% oxygen until the supply runs out or until the doctor on the emergency hotline tells you to stop delivery. If you anticipate your supply might run out, borrow some from another dive centre.

If you do run out of 100% oxygen, then have the diver continue to breathe NITROX at the highest percentage you have available.

It is critically important that this sequence of actions be followed without delay if the customer is reporting symptoms fairly soon after diving.

If they are reporting mild symptoms the following day then action is less urgent as it is unlikely that they will be seriously injured. However, you should still call the DAN hotline and the diver should absolutely not be sent out diving again.

Medical Care

The doctor on the emergency hotline may tell you that you should take the injured diver to the nearest suitable medical facility, perhaps so that oxygen delivery can be continued beyond the expected duration of your own supply or for intravenous fluids to be administered. If no doctor at this facility is specifically qualified in diving medicine then you should strongly advise the doctors to talk to the emergency hotline doctor regarding treatment.

Recompression

The emergency hotline doctor may decide that recompression of the diver is required and that you should transport the diver to the nearest recompression chamber. If you have a local recompression chamber nearby, then all your staff should be familiar with where it is, what the opening hours are and how to contact the staff. On a more general note, it is a great idea to ask the chamber staff to show you and your staff around the facilities and develop a good relationship with them. Once the diving doctor has advised recompression then getting the diver into the chamber quickly might make the difference between life and death.

Insurance Coverage

If you do not have a local recompression chamber then the hotline doctor can probably advise where the diver should be evacuated to and, at that point, the diver's insurance coverage becomes the key issue. If the diver has DAN coverage then DAN will take over the situation. If the diver has coverage with another insurer then this insurer must be contacted.

If the diver has no coverage then you need to contact the diver's family to find someone who can pay for the evacuation, which can be extremely expensive. You as the dive professional, whether you are an instructor or a dive business owner, cannot be expected to pay for this. You probably would not be able to anyway. You work in the dive industry, after all!

But it is easy to imagine a situation developing where you have an injured diver who requires evacuation and family and friends are squabbling among themselves about who is going to pay the bill and you are caught squarely in the middle of things.

Therefore, it is a very good idea to make sure that everyone who comes to dive with you has insurance coverage for an eventuality such as this. When they turn up, make sure the insurance is valid, current and sufficient. If it is not, or if they turn up without insurance, have them sign up with DAN on the spot. It is a quick procedure in most places. Until the insurance is in place, they do not dive.

You may lose a customer or two by insisting on this but, there again, are folk who can't see the need for accident and evacuation insurance when they dive really the customers you want anyway?

Practice the Procedure

Run real-life simulations to test your procedures. If there is a genuine emergency and you and your staff are doing everything for the first time, you are sure to run into unforeseen difficulties and make mistakes. For example, one dive centre decided to store all its medical oxygen in a large stand-alone 50-litre cylinder. This ensured that they had plenty of gas but unfortunately, when one day they had to transport an injured diver to the recompression chamber, they found that they couldn't get the cylinder into the car and had no smaller cylinders to use.

A common mistake that dive centres make is to assume that they only need to be prepared to deal with one casualty. However, there have been many instances when a diver gets into trouble and the buddy or dive guide gets into trouble too while trying to help. So ensure that you have enough equipment, gas and staff to deal with two injured divers simultaneously.

Resources

This chapter was written with extensive reference to Decompression Illness by John Lippmann (JL Publications Melbourne, 2011,) which is an excellent, practical and concise guide to these issues. Every dive professional should have a copy to hand in the event that one day one of your divers announces, "I think I might be bent!"

Be professional by

Developing a set procedure for suspected DCI cases.
Carrying enough O2 and delivery equipment to deal with any eventuality.
Getting to know your local chamber and its personnel.
Requiring that your customers carry insurance coverage that includes recompression treatment and evacuation.

18. Protect Your Divers and Yourself

Francis was an instructor working at a dive centre in French Polynesia. One day he picked up a couple from a nearby hotel to go diving. They had asked to do a drift dive through a pass in the reef, a site notorious for fast currents and scores of reef sharks. As always, on the way to the dive centre, Francis asked them about their diving experience and formed the impression that, although they both had a few dozen dives logged, the wife sounded confident and relaxed but the husband did not sound so sure of himself. Francis made a mental note to stay close to the husband and watch him carefully, especially during the drift dive. He considered recommending that they go somewhere else instead but he knew that they had insisted on diving the famous pass when they had called to book the day before.

On the boat, Francis noticed during the gearing up process that both of the divers had added what looked like too much weight to their weight-belts in relation to their shape and size. Instead of saying something, he gave them the benefit of the doubt, but sure enough, once they were all on the dive, drifting along at depth, he saw both divers inflate their BCDs to compensate for the excess weight, giving them a head-up-feet-down profile in the water. He decided he would mention this during the surface interval and encourage them to wear less weight on the second dive.

Staying close as planned, Francis was perfectly placed to react when the husband's weight belt came loose, slid down his legs, caught briefly on his fins and then plummeted into the depths. As he headed fast for the surface, his inflated BCD expanding as he went up, Francis grabbed hold of his leg and went up with him, trying desperately to reach his BCD dump valve to slow him down and exhaling frantically. When they reached the surface, the diver was unconscious but Francis was OK, at least for now.

He signalled the boat, helped the boat crew pull the unconscious diver in. looked around and saw that the wife had now surfaced too. Once she was safely in the boat, he called out on the radio for an ambulance to meet them at the dock and administered what first aid he could. The diver was still out cold but breathing and they had oxygen on board. Francis luckily had no symptoms of decompression illness himself.

No Hero

The injured diver was hospitalised than evacuated off the island. He eventually made a full recovery. His wife departed with him but, before flying out she was effusive in her praise for what Francis had done and told everyone who would listen that he was a hero.

Francis did not feel like a hero. Ever since the incident he had been privately kicking himself. He knew how close he had come to having a diver lose his life under his care and that he had risked incurring career threatening, if not life threatening, injuries himself. He was all too conscious of the fact that it had been his decision to take the divers out to the pass despite spotting that at least one of them might not be ready for such a difficult dive. He had also failed to intervene when he saw them wearing what looked like too much weight.

Now, the police had interviewed both him and the dive centre, their training agency had asked for an incident report, the story had made the pages of local and international newspapers and rival dive operators were making sure that plenty of harmful gossip kept circulating. No, he did not feel very heroic at all.

The diver had suffered no permanent harm and now had a new story to tell at dinner parties. However, the negative impact of the incident for both Francis and his dive centre was much longer lasting. Their reputations, locally, internationally and with their training agency had been damaged. The story would surface prominently in online searches for diving in French Polynesia and this would have an adverse effect, not only on their own business but also on scuba tourism in the region as a whole. Divers have the whole world to choose from when they plan their vacations. It does not take much bad publicity to make them look elsewhere.

How could Francis and his employers protect themselves to try to make sure that nothing similar ever happened again?

A Common Dilemma

The dilemma that Francis was faced with that morning is one that is all too familiar. Every day, dive operators all over the world take people out diving who are mostly strangers they have never seen before. To paraphrase Forrest Gump's

Momma, running a dive centre is like a box of chocolates; "you never know what you're gonna get."

To judge the level of a diver's abilities when they turn up for their dive trip, all you have to go on are the diver's word, the certification card they produce, their logbook (if you are lucky) and your intuition. These all help but they are no substitute for actually seeing someone in the water.

Many sport divers have busy lives and dive only when they are on vacation. This means that they often have long gaps between dives and during this down time their skills get rusty and their instincts and memories fade. Many people recognise this and, if they have booked a few days diving and this is the first time they have come out with you, they will usually be happy to do a checkout dive on their first day at an easy site where they can get used to the equipment again and reacquaint themselves with the underwater world.

Some dive operators also ask divers to perform a few skills during the checkout dive to demonstrate their competence. If this review points up areas where a diver needs further practice then they will assign an instructor or divemaster to work with them in a pool or off the beach before they go out diving again.

When divers understand and accept the reasons why you are asking them to do a checkout dive and skills review, then everything works perfectly. They do the dive, have a nice time and get back into the swim of things. Meanwhile, you have a chance to see how good they are, correct minor issues and make sure that the dives they do during the remainder of their stay with you match their competence. It does not guarantee that a dive accident will never happen, but it reduces the chances considerably.

Resistance

However, some divers only allocate a day or two of a holiday to diving and want to spend the other days of the trip doing other things, so they may be inclined to resent having to "waste time" doing a checkout dive rather than visiting the destination's signature sites. Having said this, if you take the time to explain the thinking behind your checkout dive policy reasonable folk will usually reach the conclusion that a check out dive is in their interests as well as yours. You can also slip in the point that a check out dive is only required when someone is diving with the company for the first time and that it will not be required when they come back again.

Unfortunately, you cannot leave it up to the divers themselves and assume that the less confident and less skilled among them will recognise their limitations themselves and actually request a check out dive. This is not necessarily because they are dishonest. It may just be that they do not have the experience to be able to judge their competence objectively. After all, the universal "great jobs" and high fives that new divers receive throughout their training are more likely to instil over-confidence than the alternative.

Some divers are strongly opposed to checkout dives, viewing them as a waste of time and money and an insult to their abilities. A glance at diver-to-diver forums shows clearly that many will actively choose operations that do not require check out dives over those that do, citing reasons such as, "I don't need to prove my skills to anyone" and "What a rip-off! I'm not going to waste money on a baby dive."

The insistence that divers demonstrate skills during the dive can even generate full-blown conflict, particularly among those who are concealing skill deficiencies and don't want to get found out, such as the people I talk about in the chapter "Masking the Problem."

So it seems clear that you can lose business by asking customers to do check out dives and this can provide sufficient justification for operators not to require them at all. Francis's experience shows the possible consequences of this but some companies will still take the risk. Scuba diving is a tough business to survive in and it is hard to say "No." Nobody ever wants to see customers walk out of the door and go off and spend money with another operator further down the beach.

Compromise

You might be tempted to compromise, to try to be flexible and forgo the check out dive requirement on the basis of a diver's elevated certification level or impressive logbook but experience suggests that this does not always work. I once had a famous course director sign up for a diving day with his teenage son. He asked me if they could go to a deep site for their first dive and requested a discount because they did not need a guide. I agreed that a check out dive would not be necessary but insisted that they take a divemaster and pay full price. It was a good thing I did. It was the divemaster who ended the dive ascending with the course director's son on his octopus after the son ran low on air. The course director himself was nowhere to be seen at the time. He later claimed that he would of course have been looking after his son if they had been alone, but as the divemaster was there, he had left it up to him, so he had something to do!

Had the son come to harm on the dive, it would have been the name of my dive centre, rather than the course director, that was dragged through the mud of Internet and industry gossip. Your customers, even if they are dive professionals themselves, spare not one thought for your business interests. Nor should you expect them to; it is their vacation, after all. This is why you have to protect yourself.

You could consider not charging your usual price for a check out dive, in an attempt to defuse the "rip off" allegations, but you still need to cover your costs. If you decide to run check out dives below cost as loss leaders, on the premise that you will recover the balance with regular dives, you must then increase your regular diving charges accordingly, factoring in the balance of the check out dive costs across however many regular dives your average customer will do.

Depending on the location of your dive centre, you can defuse any stigma attached to the check out dive by calling it an environmental familiarisation dive. That is to say; you are not saying that your new clients are not excellent, highly skilled divers but you just want to give them an easy introduction to a new diving environment. This would work well if, for instance, you are in a cool water destination and many of the new divers you get are used to warm water or if you are on a lake and your new customers are mostly ocean divers. They should still do a little skills review during the dive though.

Legal Liability

Some might argue that if a dive operator makes sure that all divers sign a liability release, then it does not matter what happens on a dive trip as the release protects the operator from liability if an accident takes place.

There is much debate over how useful releases are and I do not intend to air the arguments here. All I would say is that, no matter what your private opinion of liability releases is, you should always have every one of your divers read and sign one.

The release should be in large legible print and written in a language the diver understands fully. It should be divided into sections, each one requiring a signature, to show, as well as you can, that the diver did actually read it and did not just sign their name to the bottom of the final page.

If a diver refuses to sign the liability release then they do not get to dive with you. Notwithstanding its value as a legal document, if a diver comes to harm and it is subsequently shown that they either were not offered a liability release to sign or were not willing to sign it and then were allowed to go diving with you anyway, you come off looking unprofessional, lazy and uncaring.

No liability release will protect you from negligence. Nor will it protect you from the court of social media or from loss of business or career caused by your tarnished reputation. The best way to protect yourself as a dive instructor or dive business is always to have the safety of your divers as the number one priority. This must not be something you just advertise on your brochure, it must be the philosophy that genuinely informs everything you do. And the fact that this is your over-riding priority must be evident to all, so that if an accident happens, no-one, diver or lay-man, judge or jury, could ever accuse you of not doing your utmost to prevent the accident or of not doing everything in your power to reduce the impact for the injured diver after the accident had taken place.

Training Situations

When you are teaching divers, the best way to protect yourself is by doing things by the book. If you do not like the things a particular book asks you to do then change the book by changing your training agency. All basic diver courses have similar elements set by the industry, but there is plenty of room for diversity in the way the elements are taught.

If you teach a certification course as it is designed, following the agency standards and procedures, then your agency will support you if someone gets hurt during the course. This is one of the services you pay your annual fees for. On the other hand, if you seriously violate agency standards in training and a diver is injured or dies, then the agency will not stand by you.

In the United Kingdom, dive instructors have to teach courses following both their agency standards and guidelines set by the Government Health and Safety Executive (HSE.) In the chapter "The Value of Assistants," I describe some of the HSE diver at work guidelines in detail. Essentially, they are common-sense requirements designed to ensure that instructors exercise a reasonable duty of care towards divers under training.

Usually the instructor's own sense of professionalism and pride is sufficient to ensure that they run a course in the right way but there are always some who need a little more persuasion. When the HSE guidelines were introduced, many instructors complained because they were now required to employ safety support staff and this cut into the already slim profits they were earning from teaching.

The response from agencies and the HSE to the complaints ran along the following lines. "The requirements are universal, reasonable and achievable. If you can't run the course with the necessary personnel and make money, you need to increase the fees you charge. HSE inspectors will visit the more popular sites and conduct spot checks to ensure compliance but they cannot be everywhere at the same time. If you cut corners and there is no incident then you have got away with it. If you do it properly and there is an incident then both the HSE and your training agency will be on your side of the courtroom. But if you do not run the course according to the guidelines and there is an incident then we will be on the other side of the courtroom and you will be on your own."

Be professional by

Working always to reduce the likelihood of diver accidents to the absolute minimum.
Seeing the value of check out dives as a significant factor in pursuit of this goal.
Teaching by the book.

19. What's in the Cylinder?

It should all be completely straightforward. A customer signs up to dive with a resort. They are handed a scuba cylinder and they trust that, because they are diving with a professional operation, all the cylinder contains is air, or maybe NITROX, if that is what they have paid for. However, as the following stories illustrate, that may not always be the case.

Part 1: Water Tank?

Anna was a new diver when the incident occurred. "I was on my eighth or ninth dive ever when, after about 5 minutes and at a depth of around 13m (45ft,) I realized that my air was not coming out smoothly. I couldn't think why this should be. I had checked my pressure gauge on descent and it had shown 190bar (2850psi.) I switched to my octopus, but there was no difference. Soon the air became very thin."

"I tried to stay calm and thought for a few seconds. Everyone was going deeper and nobody was looking at me. By now the air had completely stopped and I knew something was very wrong. I held my breath. Then my husband looked around and saw that I was not following the group. He came back to me, gave me his regulator and took me up to the surface with him."

Anna's husband, an experienced instructor, takes up the story. "I had checked my wife's set up as usual pre-dive. The pressure gauge was showing 200bar (3,000psi) on the surface. I had a habit of checking on Anna frequently because she was still quite new to diving. A few minutes into the dive, I saw her hovering away from the reef in mid water, sensed something was wrong and swam towards her. She gave me a wide-eyed look and pointed at her regulator. I gave her my octopus and we went up together."

"I was puzzled as to how a full tank could become empty so quickly. It was definitely no more than 10 minutes into the dive that the incident took place and there had been no O-ring blow out. I removed the regulator from her tank after the dive then turned the valve on fully. Nothing came out. Some instinct made me turn the tank upside down and, to my surprise, and to the surprise of everyone around us, water started flowing out of the valve. I dipped my finger in it and tasted – fresh water!"

An Incredible Tale?

It seems incredible that a standard size scuba cylinder should be so full of water that a diver would only get a few minutes of air. Some might interpret the story simply as a mistake or a misunderstanding on the part of a new diver with a supportive husband.

However, when I heard the story, it brought to mind something that I came across when I ran my dive centre in Guam. We used to conduct annual visual inspections on cylinders owned by local residents and would often find a pool of water several centimetres (a couple of inches) deep in the bottom of the cylinder. This was always fresh water, not seawater. We made some enquiries and found that this is fairly common and comes from the almost universal practice in dive stores around the world of filling scuba cylinders while they are standing in a bucket or trough of water.

What happens is that the fill whips, the hoses from the compressor or air bank that you clamp onto scuba cylinders when you fill them, sometimes drop into the water while you are lifting full cylinders out of the trough and replacing them with empty ones. When the whips are then attached to the valve of empty cylinders and the airflow is turned on, the pressure of the air in the fill whips is higher than the pressure of the air in the cylinders and water droplets from the whips are driven into the cylinders. As the cylinders are filled frequently the droplets gradually accumulate and start to form little pools. As time goes on these little pools turn into bigger pools.

Bear in mind that we were in Guam, part of the USA, where a stringent system of cylinder inspections applies and is enforced by dive operators. The maximum length of time between inspections is 12 months so that means that the pools of fresh water we would find had built up in less than a year.

In many places in the world where people dive, including the island nation where Anna's dive took place, there are no regulations governing cylinder inspection, so it is not impossible that a cylinder could go for many years without anyone examining the interior. So, Anna's story may not be far-fetched after all. With her cylinder containing a large amount of fresh water, although the pressure of the air in the cylinder was high, the volume of air would have been quite small so once she started her dive she used it up very quickly. The reading on her pressure gauge must have been dropping fast during those first few minutes of her dive but she did not notice.

Why Fill in Water?

Dive centres fill scuba cylinders while they are standing in a water trough for three reasons.

1. To stop the cylinder getting too hot when they fill it fast.

2. As a convenient way to wash salt off the cylinder post dive.

3. To protect the filler from harm if the cylinder explodes during filling.

All three of these reasons reflect fuzzy thinking.

1. Filling the cylinder in water has very little impact on the cylinder temperature, partly because the water warms up as the cylinder gets hotter. The only effective way to stop a cylinder getting too hot while it is being filled is to fill it slowly and from a bank of large cool high-pressure air cylinders rather than directly from the compressor.

2. Using the fill trough to wash the salt off cylinders is ineffective as all that happens is that the water the cylinders are standing in gradually becomes saltier. Hosing the cylinders down before they are taken into the compressor room does a much better job.

3. It is true that there is a history of aluminium cylinders exploding during the filling process and when this has happened the consequences have been fatal. However, an

exploding cylinder is a bomb and no trough, whatever it is made of, is going to protect the person filling the cylinder from the effects of the explosion. Instead the decimated trough will just add more substance to the shrapnel.

Good Alloy, Bad Alloy

What is more, the risk of this happening today is much, much lower than it was several decades ago. The aluminium cylinders that exploded in the past were made from a 6351 alloy containing lead and it was the presence of lead in the alloy that created the problems that caused them to explode. Since 1988, no aluminium scuba cylinders have been made using this alloy or with any alloy containing lead. The vast majority of scuba cylinders in service today worldwide, including all cylinders made by Luxfer and Catalina, the top two manufacturers, are made from an alloy called 6061.

Although during annual inspections, cracks have occasionally been found in 6061 cylinders, none has ever exploded: and there are hundreds of millions out there.

No Need for a Bath?

It is worth making the point here that not all dive centres that fill cylinders in water are ignorant, negligent and unsafe. There are many dive centres that do this but fully recognise the potential issues and take elaborate precautions to make sure that both fill whips and cylinder valves stay dry during the process so that water does not get into their cylinders.

But if the likelihood that a scuba cylinder will explode during filling is so remote, if a water trough will not protect a filler even if a cylinder does explode, if the water is not really an effective way of removing salt or reducing the cylinder's temperature and, crucially, if the practice of wet-filling can lead to an incident such as Anna's, why do it at all?

Part 2: Scuba's Silent Killer

It was a beautiful Caribbean day, water conditions were excellent but Barbara was feeling confused. Water had started to seep into her mask and, although she knew how to clear it, somehow she was unable to get the water out. She started to ascend. Concerned, the divemaster followed her up, signaling to Pauline, the other diver in his charge, that she should wait and he would come back.

On the surface, Barbara removed her regulator, adjusted her mask, gathered her thoughts and decided she had been foolish. So, although she still did not feel well, when the divemaster swam over, she gave him the thumbs down signal, indicating that she wanted to continue with the dive, However, when they descended again, Pauline was nowhere to be found. By this time Barbara was feeling sick and disorientated again and the divemaster too was having problems.

"I was dizzy," he said afterwards. "I don't remember much, but I know my eyes closed at some point and right before we reached the surface I had a pain in my chest. I felt terrible."

So they went back up and raised the alert. A search was carried out for Pauline but she was never found. An investigation began several days later but by then the equipment the divers had used had disappeared and a medical examination of Barbara and the divemaster revealed nothing abnormal.

Although they could not be sure, given the circumstances investigators strongly suspected that the problem was caused by something in the divers' cylinders that should not have been there; one of diving's "black" gases, carbon monoxide.

Carbon Monoxide

Carbon monoxide is a completely invisible, tasteless and odourless gas that is formed when fuels such as gas, oil, coal and wood do not burn fully. It is very poisonous, has an immediately harmful effect on the respiratory system and, even in very small quantities, the consequences are potentially fatal if it gets into a scuba cylinder that someone uses for diving.

The first indication that carbon monoxide is present in a cylinder is that the diver starts to feel unwell at depth. The symptoms are headaches, irritability, dizziness, confusion and shortness of breath. The confusion is a complicating factor because it means that the diver's judgement will be impaired and therefore they may not immediately take the correct action, which is to gather the dive team immediately and abort the dive with everyone ascending together.

The reasons for carbon monoxide's high toxicity are poorly understood. It is well-known that it bonds with the haemoglobin in our bloodstream much better than oxygen, so the presence of carbon monoxide can lead to a reduction in the carriage of oxygen to body tissues. However, at mild to moderate levels this can be compensated for by an increase in blood flow so that, although the blood contains less oxygen, oxygen delivery is maintained. It seems that carbon monoxide also has other effects on cells within tissues, particularly the brain, and that these produce the toxic symptoms.

Carbon monoxide can get into a cylinder while it is being filled if there is an engine exhaust close to the compressor's air intake. The source might be the exhaust from the compressor engine itself, if it is poorly maintained or positioned in the wrong place. On a live-aboard, fumes from the boat engine when the wind is blowing the wrong way can pollute the air entering the compressor. On land, the carbon monoxide in a cylinder could come from a car with its engine running parked close to the dive shop's compressor room.

Technology Required

As a dive operator you have no way of being completely sure that there is no carbon monoxide in your cylinders without deploying a little technology. Analysers are now available that you can connect to a compressor system to warn you of its presence in the air you are pumping.

Although you may be sure that the air in your cylinders is carbon monoxide free, you may also want to reassure your divers that this is the case. You do not want everyone wandering around in your compressor room so instead you could consider having a couple of cheap hand-held carbon monoxide analysers on board the boat or in the area of the dive centre where customers pick up their cylinders so they can test the air themselves. These analysers work just like the like the oxygen analysers that measure the oxygen percentage in NITROX fills. The electro chemical sensor is user-replaceable but, unlike an oxygen sensor, it does not need periodic calibration.

Be professional by

Understanding why wet-filling cylinders is unnecessary.
Being aware of the threat of carbon monoxide.

20. Below 60 (200): A New Paradigm

Many dive professionals are drawn to deep diving and, increasingly, with all the major training agencies offering technical diver training and, consequently, a greater number of qualified deep divers around, dive operations are being called upon to run deep dives for visiting technical divers.

The concept of "deep" is changing too. Not so long ago, 40m (132ft) was considered deep but nowadays there are many divers that consider dives below 60m (200ft) to be routine. There are training parameters for teaching dives in this depth range but, to date, I have not seen a set of guidelines for how dives beyond 60m (200ft) should be run by dive operations.

This chapter seeks to address the issue by creating a new paradigm for conducting dives to such depths.

Existing Paradigms

In scuba diving there are a number of paradigms that define the way we do things. The paradigms change or shift as conditions or circumstances dictate. Depth is a crucial factor in creating a need for paradigm shift. As we go deeper, we dive differently and different procedures apply. You should not approach a dive to 40m (132ft) in the same way that you approach a dive to 12m (40ft).

Other major elements that lead to a paradigm change in scuba diving are altitude and an overhead environment but in this chapter I will concentrate simply on concerns of depth.

The sport diving depth safety limits are well known: around 18m (60ft) for a new diver and around 39m (130ft) for no decompression diving on a single cylinder. Of course, depth limits and other diving procedures are often presented by training agencies as rules but they are really guidelines, not rules.

The limits were set at the dawn of recreational scuba diving, since when the equipment and technology available to divers have improved but the limits have not changed. Indeed they have become more or less set in stone. Some training agencies play around with the numbers a little, some anarchists rail against them but generally speaking they are universally accepted.

The reason for this is that these limits actually work. They make sense. Each one marks a depth beyond which, primarily because of gas physics and human physiology, divers need to change the way they dive.

Let's look at the paradigms we have already in a little more detail.

Down to 18m (60ft)

At 18m (60ft) and shallower, there is little chance of new divers incurring mandatory decompression before they run low on air and even less chance if they are using NITROX. Also, their minds are unlikely to be affected by narcosis.

However, beyond 18m(60ft) narcosis is definitely present and can affect divers' concentration, a particularly significant problem when diving is new to them and they have not yet learned the basic skills to the point of instinct.

Remove the threats posed by narcosis, running out of air and going into deco and you remove much of the risk that a new diver, properly trained, will come to harm. So, the section of the water column from the surface down to 18m (60ft) works as a zone in which divers can safely get used to the underwater world, gain confidence and build familiarity with equipment and diving techniques.

Once they are comfortable with the basic skills and used to monitoring their air supply and no decompression time, they can then go deeper with confidence.

Down to 39m (130ft)

Scuba diving's safety record suggests that an experienced diver on a single cylinder with good, instinctive skills can function quite safely in open water at depths shallower than 39m (130ft) following the standard sport diving paradigm set out in countless training manuals over the years. Yes, using doubles is safer and, yes, it depends on the conditions, but the historical record speaks for itself.

Once you go deeper than 39m (130ft) you quickly enter the realm of compulsory decompression stops and this is not a place you want to be if you only have one source of air and no back up supply to resort to in the event of a free-flowing regulator or a blown o-ring.

The water column beyond 39m (130ft) also exposes a diver to higher levels of narcosis requiring greater awareness and training.

Beyond 39m (130ft)

This is where the new paradigm that was introduced by technical diving pioneers in the late 1980s and early 1990s comes in. It involves a range of procedures, decompression tables and equipment innovations that give divers the ability to explore safely beyond 39m (130ft).

A trained technical diver using air as a bottom mix in a standard set of double cylinders and equipped with a single cylinder of decompression gas can accomplish dives with minimal risk much deeper than 39m (130ft). But, once armed with the standard technical diving skills, knowledge and gear, is this diver then able to dive safely to dive to any depth?

This is an especially important issue to consider today when the boundaries between recreational diving and technical diving are becoming blurred and technical diving is increasingly viewed as merely an extension of the sport rather than a completely different discipline.

For dives to depths between 39m and 60m (140ft and 200ft), it is easy to see why and how technical diving is merging with the mainstream. Ascent and decompression times are relatively short, you can complete the dive safely on your bottom gas in an emergency, you only need one decompression gas and now that wings, harnesses, surface marker buoys and the like are increasingly being adopted by even new sport divers, the transition from one type of equipment to another is not as abrupt as it used to be.

But deeper than this, there is nothing mainstream about the way you have to dive. Beyond 60m (200ft,) very different procedures for scuba diving are required

Beyond 60m (200ft)

Why do I choose 60m (200ft)? After all, many training agencies now set shallower depth limits such as 51m (170ft) or 55m (184ft), for technical diving courses using air as the deep gas which, as you will see, is one of the key elements of this particular paradigm shift. Setting shallower depth limits for air diving reflects admirable conservative tendencies on the part of the training agencies, but, as I mentioned before, I believe the reason why 18m (60ft) and 39m (130ft) have lasted as scuba diving depth limits is that they mark points where primarily because of gas physics and human physiology, divers must, for reasons of survival, change the way they dive. The depth of 60m (200ft) meets this requirement too.

So what are the five principal factors that characterise the paradigm for diving below 60m (200ft?)

1. You Don't Use Air

Beyond 60m (200ft), air presents a diver with a number of problems that, taken together, form an insurmountable obstacle that rules out air for safe diving at such depths.

The first problem with air is oxygen, a gas that we need to sustain life but which can also harm us if we consume too much. In large doses oxygen makes us convulse uncontrollably and if a diver gets oxygen-induced convulsions underwater he will probably drown without a calm, expert team member nearby to help.

At the surface, the air we breathe from a scuba cylinder has a harmless partial pressure of 0.21 atmospheres but if we breathe from the same cylinder at a depth beyond 60 m (200ft), the oxygen partial pressure rises to beyond 1.5 ATA, the generally accepted maximum safe level for a swimming diver.

The second problem with using air is that it is dense and, like all gasses, it becomes denser as its pressure increases. This means that at depth it becomes more difficult to breathe. Breathing on scuba at depth is made even more difficult by the fact that we have to bring this dense gas into our lungs and expel it again via artificial apparatus (our regulators) while the pressure of the water around us is pressing in on our bodies. This can lead to a third problem.

The third problem is carbon dioxide (CO_2) build up or hypercapnia. The primary consequence of the reduced efficiency caused by breathing dense air through artificial apparatus is that we retain more CO_2 in our lungs and bloodstream. This not only makes us even more susceptible to oxygen toxicity convulsions, it can also trigger our automatic emergency response system, the final phase of which is panic, the diver's worst enemy.

The anxiety induced by a build-up of CO_2 can sneak up on an unprepared diver and override all intellect and reason. Underwater, a trained deep diver thinking logically will sense what is happening and respond correctly. He will stop everything he is doing, relax, take a series of deep full breaths in and out and clear his head.

However, there is a final issue that makes it very difficult for a diver below 60m (200ft) to think logically. This is narcosis, which at such depths can be completely debilitating and render you incapable of rational thought.

So, on a dive on air below 60m (200ft) these four factors combine to present divers with a scenario where

1. They are at risk of an oxygen-induced convulsion.

2. They are finding it more difficult to breathe.

3. Chemically engendered panic is hovering dangerously close by.

4. And they are not thinking clearly.

Furthermore, the problems are multiplying: the increased density of their breathing gas causes them to retain more CO_2 and the build up of CO_2 is both increasing the risk of an oxygen toxicity hit and adding to the narcosis they are experiencing.

This is why you cannot safely use air below 60m (200ft).

You Use Helium

Legendary figures such as Sheck Exley, Bill Hamilton, Tom Mount and Billy Deans were responsible for bringing helium based gases into the realm of sport diving and helium has been by far the most significant factor in making deep sport diving safer over the past 25 years.

It is a very light, non-toxic, minimally narcotic gas. By adding it to our breathing mixture for deep dives, we can reduce the percentage of oxygen and thus reduce the risk of oxygen toxicity. It also makes the overall mixture less dense than air, making it easier for us to breathe and making us less prone to hypercapnia. Furthermore, it reduces the percentage of narcotic gases in the mix, which means we dive with a much clearer head. The only disadvantage as far as the sport diver is concerned is that helium is expensive and not easily available everywhere.

In commercial diving and military circles, they have known for a long time that adding helium to breathing gas has huge physiological advantages for a diver working at depth. The breathing gas of choice for their deep divers is a mixture of oxygen and helium only, known as HELIOX. They use a very high percentage of helium because the primary concern is to minimize narcosis in the working diver and the consideration of cost is secondary to getting the job done.

As sport divers, we do not have the luxury of vast funds. But, then again, when we dive we are usually just sightseeing and are not engaged on work that requires intense concentration. So we feel we can deal with a little narcosis and add only as much helium as we need to keep the amount of oxygen in the breathing mix within safe limits and keep the level of narcosis manageable. This gives us a mixture of oxygen, nitrogen and helium that we call Heliair or TRIMIX.

I mentioned the cost of helium. On dives below 60m, you must use helium and you must use as much as the dive plan requires. There are no short cuts, no poor man's options. I dived for a time with a TRIMIX diver who wanted to do a series of build up dives to culminate in a flagship 150m (500ft) dive that he was planning. As the dives got deeper, instead of following standard operating procedure and staying on a helium based gas on ascent until he reached NITROX depths, he decided to try to save money, switch to a cylinder of air at

60m (200ft) and use this until he made his first NITROX switch at 40 m (132ft).

I still remember clearly what happened when, at 60m (200ft) on the way up from a preparatory 120m (400ft) dive, he made the switch from TRIMIX to air. It was as if he had just walked into a wall. His eyes became vacant and he just stopped all movement. He was virtually comatose. I swam over, waved his TRIMIX regulator in front of his face and after what seemed like an age, he took it and put it in his mouth. His eyes began to clear after a few breaths and we continued the dive.

He didn't repeat the experiment.

If you cannot afford to do the dive safely, do not do the dive. The amount of money you save is the value you place on your life. Not all TRIMIX dives are ruinously expensive. You can always recycle your reserve TRIMIX supply from one deep dive and use it with an air top-up to do a subsequent shallower dive.

2. You Need More Than 2 Gasses

On any dive below 60m (200ft), the oxygen percentage in your bottom gas will be lower than 21% in order to prevent oxygen toxicity at depth. In most cases it will have such a low oxygen percentage (below 16%) that it will not be breathable at the surface. So, on the boat, you cannot just put your bottom mix regulator in your mouth and jump in. If you do, the low oxygen level will cause you to black out as you hit the water.

Instead, you need to enter the water breathing from another gas, usually a light 32% to 40% NITROX. For the descent portion of the dive, this is known as your travel gas. As soon as you reach a depth where your bottom gas becomes breathable you switch regulators and start breathing from the bottom gas. You then shut off the valve of your travel gas and tuck the travel gas regulator away tidily. You do this so that it is impossible to lose the contents via a leaky regulator at depth. This is important because you are going to need your remaining travel gas later during your ascent when it becomes your first decompression gas.

I say "first" because beyond 60m (200ft) you also need multiple decompression gasses and lots of decompression gas. The bottom gas mixture that keeps you alive at depth contains a lot of inert gas (helium and nitrogen) but very little oxygen. To try to complete the dive safely on this mixture would require many hours of decompression and a vast amount of gas, far more than any diver could ever carry. So, as you ascend you need to stop breathing it as soon as it is safe to do so and start breathing a gas with a higher oxygen content and a lower inert gas content. This helps your body release more quickly the helium and nitrogen that have built up in your tissues and bloodstream while you were at depth. It also reduces your decompression time to a manageable level. Once you get up into the shallows, you then switch to oxygen or a very rich 75% to 80% NITROX for your final long decompression stops.

Of course, carrying different gases for different phases substantially increases the number of things that can go wrong on a dive. Loss of decompression gas is potentially fatal which is why smart divers keep it attached to them at all times. Also, deep divers always need to bear in mind that they are carrying three or more different gases, any of which can kill them if they put the wrong regulator in their mouth at the wrong depth. To echo a point I made earlier, there is nothing mainstream about that and this is another good reason why a paradigm shift at 60m (200ft) is so essential.

3. You Need A Team

Nobody should ever dive beyond 60m (200ft) without a support team. Even if a diver chooses to solo dive for the deep portion of the dive, in water and surface support is mandatory. There is no valid counter argument for this. Just go through the "What Ifs." For example, "what if I forget to shut off the valve on my final deco cylinder and while I am at depth my regulator fails and the contents just flow out unnoticed into the water?" If this happens on a 50m (165ft) dive on air you just use your bottom mix reserve and do a longer decompression. Below 60m (200ft), if you have nobody to bring you replacement decompression gas, there is a good chance that you will not survive the dive. And nothing should ever be left to chance, good or otherwise.

The most important part of this sort of dive is the decompression phase and this is where the deep divers are most likely to require help. Therefore, this is also where support teams and dive operators running deep dives need to concentrate their efforts. Whoever they are, however experienced they are, there are things the deep divers cannot do themselves because they are trapped by their decompression burden. Their movements and options are strictly curtailed because they cannot descend without increasing their decompression time and gas needs and they cannot ascend beyond their decompression ceiling without increasing the risk of decompression illness.

Spare decompression gas can always be staged on the planned decompression route, be it an ascent line, a reef wall or a purpose-built station. But by far the safest way of ensuring a successful deep diving operation is to have at least one experienced pair of eyes actually in the water. This pair of eyes should belong to a trained technical dive supervisor.

In the 1990s, when technical diving was still in its infancy, I had no shortage of volunteer safety divers to call on to assist me on deep training and fun dives. However, I soon got tired of bringing my team up the wall to the appointed meet and greet location only to find nobody there because the safety divers had got bored and had gone off to look at some fish. So I decided I needed to train a team of specialists.

The Most important People in the Water

Ideally, technical dive supervisors need to be so well trained and experienced that they can identify problematic situations before the divers themselves realise that they are in difficulty. These might include a diver who has inadvertently switched to the wrong gas on ascent or a diver with a BCD problem who is finding it difficult to maintain decompression stop depth.

The supervisors are responsible for setting up the decompression station and back up decompression gas on the planned ascent route but they must also be ready to make alternative arrangements at short notice in case the deep divers have been unable to ascend along the planned route and are coming up elsewhere. This consideration means that they must always to be able to surface and communicate with the boat if necessary so they need to have the awareness and discipline not to go into decompression themselves.

Obviously, good teamwork and communications are crucial, both underwater between the dive supervisors and the deep dive team and on the surface between the supervisors and the boat crew. Classic communication devices are slates, hand signals and different coloured surface marker buoys to say, "here we are" or "problem send gas." Today, the small VHF radios (Nautilus Lifeline and the like) that I mention elsewhere in Scuba Professional are absolutely essential equipment for any team running deep dives in open water locations where 2 to 3 hour dive times can easily lead to divers being lost at sea.

4. You Take No Passengers

When you are running this sort of diving, everyone needs to be focussed on the operation. Ideally, you would run deep dives from a separate boat with a dedicated team but if this is not possible then you must avoid giving the supervisory team other duties that might distract them from the task in hand.

Everyone on the dive and on the supervisory team must also be fully trained to the level of the dive. There is no room for passengers. This story illustrates the point perfectly.

Bob was hired for a deep-water treasure hunt. One bright morning he was assigned to do metal finding runs with a magnetometer on a sand pit at around 75m (250ft) and was preparing his gear when the boss came over to say that he would have company on the dive. A top instructor from a local dive centre that was helping bankroll the operation would be tagging along. The boss said that the instructor was not TRIMIX trained but that he had briefed him fully, he had put his equipment together for him and he had told the instructor to stick close to Bob while he worked, ascend with him when he had finished and just copy whatever Bob did on the ascent.

Bob introduced himself to the instructor and led him through the dive plan. He seemed calm, confident and capable, said he had done a huge number of dives on this site in the past, albeit much shallower, and not to worry about him.

"OK," thought Bob, "I won't!"

It all went well until about 25 minutes into the dive, when something made Bob look up and he saw his new buddy swimming fast towards him, frantically slicing his forearm over his throat. Bob put the magnetometer down, stretched out his arm to fend the diver off and offered him his long hose regulator with the other hand. While he was gulping down gas and getting his head back together, Bob checked his doubles. They were empty!

Bob shot his "need gas" buoy up and started a gas-sharing ascent. At 40m (132ft) he handed the diver over to a technical dive supervisor and eventually everyone surfaced safe and sound. However, at the debrief that evening the team made a solemn pact: "no more TRIMIX intros, ever!"

5. You Need a Cave Diving Mind-set

The mind-set required to conduct dives below 60m (200ft) needs to be similar to that required for cave diving, a discipline in scuba diving that has thankfully resisted all attempts to ally it with the mainstream. On a deep TRIMIX dive the sunlight may be visible as you are on the way up but you are often 2 or 3 hours away from feeling it directly on your skin. The situation deep divers are in can be looked at as a "virtual" overhead environment. From a survival point of view, they might as well be in the darkness of a flooded cave and far away from the nearest exit.

This mind-set is the primary thing that Bob's "passenger" was missing. He had thousands of dives logged, was supremely confident and comfortable in the water but was just not used to this type of diving. He did not possess the paranoia that all cave divers and deep TRIMIX divers must have always lurking at the edge of their minds. He did not know how quickly you use up your gas at over 8 atmospheres and when this realisation dawned on him, he experienced an unprecedented level of stress and this quickly turned into panic, causing him to breathe through his gas even more quickly.

Everyone involved in executing dives below 60m (200ft) needs to have levels of self-discipline and team discipline far beyond those normally required in sport diving. They need to have the mental strength to concentrate intently for long periods of time when not much is happening but be ready at any moment to deal with an emergency. They need constantly to be on the alert for events or situations that might increase the risk of the dive and have the presence of mind and courage to abort a dive when they believe they perceive a threat to the team's safety and move to shallower depths to live to dive another day.

Be professional by

Adopting a five point paradigm for dives beyond 60m.
1. Helium
2. Multiple Deco Gasses
3. Technical Dive Supervisors
4. No Passengers and
5. A Cave Diving Mind-set.

§4

Developing Scuba's Safety Culture

21. Detecting and Dealing with Stress

It is something that every dive-master or dive guide experiences at least once; that heart-stopping moment when a diver in your charge suddenly bolts for the surface. You assemble the other divers to accompany you or you leave them in the care of an assistant and you ascend slowly, praying that the diver who bolted is OK and cursing yourself for not spotting earlier that they had a problem.

You have done at least one thing correctly though. You have resisted the urge to chase them to the surface, knowing that, once a diver bolts, their own impetus along with expanding air makes it impossible to reach them and by going up quickly yourself to try and catch them, you risk turning one problem into two.

You also have a responsibility to make sure the other divers in your group are alright before you deal with the diver who has bolted; they might have seen what happened and become nervous themselves. If you then suddenly disappear they might start to panic too.

In many cases, you reunite with the panicked diver on the surface and thankfully they are fine. They had the presence of mind or the instinct to breathe out and vent their BCD as they ascended. But you know from your experience and training what could have happened and that you might have had a seriously injured diver on your hands. For many nights afterwards you lie in bed wondering how you did not see the problem coming.

The most important things that dive professionals need to learn is how to identify stress in ourselves, recognise it in others and handle it when it occurs. If stress is not controlled early on it can lead to panic, and when people panic they usually respond in a way that makes the situation worse, such as bolting for the surface. In scuba-diving panic is a life threatening event and the major cause of diving fatalities worldwide.

It may well be that you did not notice the signs of impending panic in the diver you were looking after because during the dive you were distracted by thinking about how to deal with problems in your own life, money, girlfriend, boyfriend, family issues, whatever. Your own stress can make you blind to signs of stress in other people.

So the first rule as soon as you put on your dive-master / dive guide or instructor "hat," is that you must put everything else behind you and give 100% of your attention to the divers in your care.

Having done this, you can then focus on your divers. How are they feeling? Have they got previous experience of the sort of diving you are going to do today or is this something new for them? When did they last dive? Are they using new equipment?

All this information and more can be obtained by chatting easily with them as they arrive and get their gear ready. I used to brief our hotel pick-up guys to talk to divers during the drive to the boat, not only to be friendly and put them at their ease but also to see if there were any concerns the dive team should know about in advance.

When the pick-up guys arrived at the boat, they would pass on the information to the dive team who could then make last minute changes to the plan for the day or re-arrange staff responsibilities accordingly.

You can use your boat and dive briefings to defuse many of the potential concerns and much of the apprehension. Anticipate what the divers might be worried about, for example fast currents, cold water or poor visibility, and explain what steps you will be taking to minimise the problems these conditions can cause.

You might also consider adopting and introducing divers to visualisation and the in-water check, a couple of stress prevention strategies that technical divers use before big dives but can be valuable tools for everyone and are rarely taught in initial courses.

Visualisation

After the boat briefing, encourage the divers to find a quiet place to sit on their own or with their buddy on the way to the dive-site, where they can sit and remove all thoughts from their minds concerning whatever is going on in their lives elsewhere and think only about the dive ahead.

They should reflect on your briefing and review what they have researched about the site or what they remember from previous dives there. Counsel them to think positive thoughts, imagine all the cool things they are going to see and visualise a successful dive.

They should picture themselves relaxed and in control, maintaining a steady breathing rate and good buoyancy, checking their computer and SPG frequently, staying in touch with the dive team and finally making a slow, safe and controlled ascent with a safety stop, ending the dive with plenty of air remaining.

Visualising the dive and thinking about what is about to take place and how to deal with it builds self-confidence and puts a diver in a relaxed, positive, forward-looking frame of mind, the exact sort of attitude that everyone should have before any endeavour.

But this is not the only benefit. It is often the case that a positive visualisation before a dive will remove feelings of apprehension. Apprehension is best defined as a feeling of uncertainty about your ability to cope with a situation. The principal danger of divers embarking on a dive when they are apprehensive is that apprehension can build and turn into full-blown panic in the event of even a minor emergency.

Visualisation can also help divers identify problems in advance or warn them of any aspects of the dive that they may not be comfortable with and that they can then share with you. Maybe they will realise during their visualisation of the ascent that they have forgotten their surface marker buoy. Far better to remember that before the dive than when they reach for it later!

The In-Water Check

All divers learn the pre-dive safety check during their beginners' course and this soon becomes something they do instinctively. Another really good habit you can teach your students is to perform an in-water check right at the start of their dive. The whole process of gearing up on a busy boat, entering the water and descending can be rushed and stressful and it can undo all the positive effects of any pre-dive visualization.

So encourage them, once they have left the surface and are a couple of metres / few feet under water, surrounded by the peace and quiet of the ocean, to pause, take a few seconds to compose themselves, get a long, slow, deep breathing cycle going and make sure all their equipment is intact, buckles are fastened, nothing is leaking and their gauges are working.

Then they can set off calmly for the depths.

Controlling Stress on the Dive

Even if a diver has prepared perfectly, there is always the possibility that stress can occur during a dive. The most common forms are time pressure stress from having a limited air supply and compounded stress from task loading. An example of compounded stress is the feeling of inadequacy that can arise when a diver is managing an underwater camera and dive light on a night dive while controlling buoyancy and trying to keep in touch with the rest of the team all at the same time.

Careful observation and managing the speed of your group can ensure that these stressors do not escalate into panic. Having an assistant makes this much easier. It is very useful to have additional pairs of eyes to help you keep track of larger groups and on night dives, when divers are less likely to stay together.

Monitoring Air Supply

A common cause of the type of panicked ascent I referred to at the beginning of this chapter is a diver running out of air or belatedly checking their gauge, finding they are dangerously low on air and deciding that the surface is the best place to be. For this reason, you always need to have an idea of how much air your divers have.

Of course, a good way of finding this out is to ask them and, with very new divers, issuing frequent reminders that they should check their gauge are an excellent way of embedding this crucial habit into their psyche.

With more experienced divers, however, overtly checking how much air they have left can irritate them and cause resentment. This does not mean that it is any less necessary. More experienced divers often become complacent. So you need to be more subtle and exercise a little cunning.

A useful trick to help you monitor how much air your divers have left without constantly going around asking them to show you their SPGs is to spot something cool to show them about 10 minutes into the dive. Once they are all crowding round to look at it, circle behind them and take a sneaky look at how much air they each have left. See who has used most and then you will know which diver you have to keep an eye on, in the certain knowledge that the others will always have more left than him, (it is usually a him!)

Taking this tactic one step further, you can do a little mental arithmetic to estimate how long into the dive he is likely to run low. If he has used 30bar (450psi) in 10 minutes and the group stays at around the same depth, then he will be have used 150bar (2250psi) and be down to 50bar (750psi) after 50 minutes.

Another way of working out how much air your target diver has throughout the dive without checking on him is to compare his consumption after 10 minutes with your own. If he used 20bar (300psi) in the first 10 minutes and you used 10bar (150psi) in the same time then by the time you have used 50bar (750psi) he will have used 100 bar (1500psi;) and so on.

Of course this is not an exact science and you need to be conservative. You should be alert too for changes in breathing patterns; a lazy, out of shape diver with good buoyancy going with the flow and sipping his air may suddenly become a panting, gas guzzling monster if the current drops or shifts direction!

If, instead of SPGs, your divers are using wrist-mounted computers with integrated air supply monitoring via a sender screwed into the regulator high pressure port, then it is more difficult to spy on them. If you think it is not appropriate to badger them constantly for their air reading, a reliable tell-tale sign that someone is going through their air quickly is frequent exhalations. Sometimes it almost looks like a continuous stream.

Physical Consequences of Stress

Stress can manifest itself in strange ways. I once employed an excellent instructor who had no difficulties at all when he was working as part of a team. However, when he was asked to guide or teach a group of divers on his own he was never able to equalize adequately on descent and therefore always had to cancel the dive.

This was obviously a serious impediment to the instructor's plans for making a career in scuba diving so he sought expert medical advice to find out if there was an underlying cause for his strange problem. It turned out that the issue was one of confidence and responsibility.

When the instructor was working alone, a subconscious anxiety that he was not capable of adequately looking after the divers in his charge manifested itself as a physical inability to equalize, which prevented him from diving and removed the problem. When he had someone with him to share the burden of responsibility he was no longer anxious and therefore had no difficulty equalizing and diving.

After a period of counselling, the issue disappeared completely and, as far as I know, he is still working very competently in diving today.

References

The identification and management of stress is an important topic that does not always receive the attention it should in diver training materials. If you are interested in learning more I recommend the excellent, thought provoking and highly readable book "Stress and Performance in Diving" by Arthur Bachrach and Glen Egstrom. Well worth looking at also is the "Psychological Aspects and Survival Strategies" chapter in "The Tao of Survival Underwater" by Tom Mount and others.

Be professional by

Encouraging divers to adopt stress-prevention strategies.
Deploying strategies to monitor divers and anticipating stressful situations before they occur.
Being aware that stress can have physical consequences.

22. The Threat of Complacency

Complacency is a risk for all dive professionals face and it can be insidious. You do not see it sneaking up on you until one day it takes you by surprise and an incident takes place that makes you realise suddenly that you are no longer the careful, conscientious diver that you once were or that some of the things you thought you knew about scuba diving were completely wrong.

Here are two true stories that illustrate the problem perfectly.

Story One: It Can't Happen to Me!

This is Amy's tale.

I am an instructor and professional dive guide. I have been diving for 12 years and have logged well in excess of 2500 dives in that time. Last month I was diving off a day-boat in Dumaguete in the Philippines. It was the first dive of the day; I slipped my gear on in the boat, did my usual checks and back-rolled into the water. I had a problem descending at first so I exhaled a little more fully than usual, ducked headfirst below the surface and kicked down to a depth where the water pressure would compress my wetsuit a little and make me more negatively buoyant. That worked so I headed on down.

The dive was a muck dive on a sand slope and I was concentrating as usual on trying to find stuff to show my divers. Twenty five minutes into the dive at a depth of around 30m (100ft,), my tank valve started banging into my head which was a bit annoying so I took my gear off, adjusted my tank strap, pulled it higher and slipped back into my BCD.

I was now finding it hard to breathe from the regulator. "It's OK," I thought, "not a problem, I can manage." I tried switching to my octopus but it breathed hard too so I switched back to my primary second stage. Then I checked my air, not thinking that there might be a problem; just making my normal occasional check. And the needle was at zero!

I thought, "hmm, I need a buddy." There was one, taking pictures nearby. I swam over and tried to get his attention by tapping him on the shoulder. He signalled "wait" without looking up. So I waited and then tapped him on the shoulder again, a bit more insistently this time and, when he looked at me I indicated that I was out of air. He looked surprised but took the regulator out of his mouth, handed it to me, switched to his alternate second stage then double-checked my gauge and valve. His eyes widened in surprise. "Yes, that's right," I thought "I told you I was out of air."

We exchanged "lets' go up" signals and started moving slowly up the slope. My new buddy had a 2m (6ft) hose on his primary second stage so we could swim freely and side-by-side. Because we were so relaxed and he had plenty of air for both of us, we made a very slow, controlled ascent and did an extended stop at 4.5m (15ft) before surfacing.

Of course, when I got back to the dive centre my first mission was to find out what had happened. Apparently, the staff on the boat had not changed my cylinder overnight and I had gone into the water with the 80bar (1200psi) or so remaining from my last dive of the previous day.

Of course, although the dive centre had made a mistake, the responsibility for me running out of air was mine alone, completely. I thought I always checked my air before going in the water and frequently during the dive. I obviously do not do this! My air always lasts me a long time and I never run out before the rest of the group I am diving with so over the years, it seems I have unconsciously lost the habit.

Also, apart from not checking my gauge I completely missed a number of warning signs. The reason I had difficulty making my initial descent was that the air in my tank was low and therefore it was more buoyant than usual. My tank valve was banging against the back of my head because the tank was floating up as I used up my remaining air and it became positively buoyant.

Finally, I started to have difficulty breathing because the air pressure in the tank had dropped to a level below the 13 Bar (200 psi) needed to enable the regulator to work properly at that depth.

Looking back on the episode later, I wondered why, despite several warning signs, it did not dawn on me earlier that I was dangerously low on air. I can only think that it was a combination of narcosis at depth slowing down my thought processes and my subconscious (and misplaced) confidence that, with all my experience, I could never have an air supply problem.

I also reflected on some of the factors that turned what could have been a major problem into a minor inconvenience. I kept calm; my buddy was close by and had plenty of air for both of us and the extra-long hose on his regulator meant we could swim up together easily without getting in each other's way. Making the ascent from 30m (100ft) having to stay pressed up against my buddy while breathing from a short hose would have been very uncomfortable and the lack of freedom of movement would have made me highly stressed.

Unsurprisingly, I have now made a couple of changes to the way I dive. I now have a much longer hose on my octopus and I have adopted a new pre-dive routine that I intend to stick to religiously.

Story Two: Running Out Fast!

Ben is a master instructor and this was his experience on a recent dive in South Komodo, Indonesia.

It was the first dive of the day; I rolled backwards into the ocean from our little tender boat, descended to 24m (80ft,) swam over to Cannibal Rock and began a gentle exploration from the bottom up. Even at this hour of the morning the colours were glorious, there were battalions of fish and the huge rock was visible in all its splendour in clear warm water.

15 minutes into the dive, at around 18m (60ft) I simultaneously felt and heard a massive explosion, the pressure wave battering me from above. My first (illogical) thought was that I had been fish-bombed. After all we were in remote South-east Asia and it has happened to me before. It was only when the thunderous noise did not stop that it occurred to me that this

was no bomb. I concluded (correctly this time) that a catastrophic air supply failure must have just taken place somewhere behind my head.

The next few thoughts, actions and decisions came fast. I looked at my pressure gauge, which was already down to 100bar (1500psi) and falling fast. I could actually see the needle moving. My first thought was to slip my BCD off and bring it round to the front so I could discover what had happened and see if I could deal with it myself. But I was completely thrown by the speed at which the needle on my gauge was dropping. I knew I would not have time to do that before I ran out of air completely.

I realised I was going to need some help. The other divers in my group were not too far away and I swam towards them. The first one I came across was Martin but he was burdened by a monster video system and I remembered that his "octopus" was an inflator hose regulator - no good going to him. Behind Martin was Kate, but she was also carrying a big camera and was head-down, legs in the air, no doubt photographing something tiny camouflaged in something spiny as usual - so not her either. Then I saw Cecile, an experienced diver armed with an octopus regulator on a 1.5m (5ft) hose - perfect. So I politely asked if I might share air with her, she generously acquiesced, we ascended comfortably together and I survived to tell the tale.

When I got back on board the boat I found that there was a small cut in the valve face O-ring. It had probably been showing signs of damage for a while, allowing a little high-pressure air to bubble past it gently, but I had not even noticed. However, when it failed it got my complete attention! I had seen an O-ring blow before a dive many times but had never experienced it underwater.

I had always thought that I would be able to deal with anything that happened to me on a dive but I didn't expect to have so little time. So I did some research and found an article in Advanced Diver Magazine, which had run a number of tests to see how long divers actually have to react if they have an air supply issue.

They found that if a high-pressure hose fails, it will take 22 minutes for a scuba cylinder to empty completely, but if a low pressure hose bursts or there is a valve or first stage failure then the cylinder will go from 207bar (3,000psi) to zero in less than 90 seconds. Even a free-flowing regulator will empty a full cylinder in less than 3 minutes. I just had no idea. If I had been asked, I would have said that a high-pressure hose problem would be much more serious than a free-flowing regulator. How wrong I was!

What do I do differently now? I replace all O-rings as soon as I notice bubbles. I don't dive alone with a single cylinder and I always make sure I have an alternate source of air for deep dives.

I also try to keep myself much better informed about my profession and do not assume that I know everything.

Be professional by

Being aware of the threat of complacency.
Not relaxing your guard.
Looking out for gaps in your knowledge.
Repairing the gaps when you find them.

23. Constructive Paranoia

It is unusual for a chapter in a scuba diving book to begin in the highlands of Papua New Guinea but that is exactly where this one begins. It will be a while before I get around to actually talking about diving but bear with me. I hope you see where I am going as we move along.

A few decades ago, a young ornithologist was on an expedition in the highlands of Papua New Guinea, leading a team of New Guineans. They spent the first few days climbing through the forest until they reached the level where they were to spend a few days studying birds. The young ornithologist selected a site for their camp beneath a huge forest tree, its bark covered in thick moss. He asked his companions to build a sleeping platform but they became agitated and told him they would not spend the night there. He asked "Why?" and they told him that the tree was dead and they were afraid it might fall on the camp during the night and kill them.

He tried to reason with them. The site looked perfect to him and, albeit dead, the tree looked very solid. But they were adamant in their refusal and eventually they all agreed on a different camping site far away from the tree. Later, the young ornithologist admitted that at the time he felt annoyed. He thought the New Guineans were exaggerating the danger to a ridiculous degree. However, over the following months, as he continued his research, he realised that at least once a day he would hear the noise of a tree falling in the forest and at night he would listen to his companions recounting stories of people who had been killed by falling trees.

A Little Maths

After a while, he did the maths. He estimated that New Guineans spent about 100 nights a year camping in the forest. Over a lifetime of several decades that would amount to several thousand nights. Even if the probability of a tree falling on you and killing you on any given night is very low, the more time you spend in the forest the more likely it is that you will become a victim. The New Guineans cannot avoid the risk of falling trees by not going into the forest. After all, they need to go into the forest to find food and to get from one place to another. But they can certainly minimise the risk by not camping underneath a dead tree.

The ornithologist noticed that safety in general was a major theme around the campfires at night. He also saw how tales of how people had come to harm or just avoided disaster particularly fascinated the children and guessed that they constituted an important part of their education. He concluded that the obsession with safety was an essential cultural survival tool that contributed significantly to keeping the community safe and labelled it "constructive paranoia."

The World Until Yesterday

The young ornithologist was Jared Diamond and today he is a celebrated and much-published academic and author. I found the falling trees story in his book "The World Until Yesterday", in which he looks at the few tribal societies remaining today and examines their behaviour, procedures and strategies.

In the same book, Diamond also describes a trip he took in a small outrigger boat between islands in northwest Indonesian Papua, the famed divers' mecca of Raja Ampat. To cut a long story short, the journey began late in the afternoon, the cargo was poorly loaded, it shifted while the boat was being driven too fast, water came on board faster than the crew could bale it out and the boat ultimately sank. Diamond and eight other passengers were afloat in the open ocean for a couple of hours until, just before sunset, they were lucky enough to be spotted and picked up by a passing fishing vessel.

At first, he was very angry with the crew for endangering his life and those of the other passengers. However, a few days later, he fell into conversation with a local man and told the tale of his near miss. "I was also there that day," answered the Papuan. "I was planning to take that boat too but when I saw how careless the crew were and considered how late in the day it was, I decided to wait and take another boat the following morning."

This caused Diamond to pause and reflect. He remembered in hindsight that, despite the fact that he was in Papua, none of the passengers on board his boat had actually been Papuan. He had noticed before boarding that the boat crew were laughing and joking around and apparently not focussed on their work, but he had not considered that their careless behaviour could actually pose a threat to his safety. He had failed to look at the situation with a constructive paranoia mind-set as the Papuan man had done and had nearly paid for it with his life.

Technical Divers

Any technical divers reading this will immediately get what Jared Diamond is writing about. Although they may not use the actual phrase, technical divers employ constructive paranoia as a survival technique. They address the real risks of diving up front. They know how the technical divers who went before them got hurt and have developed procedures and equipment to reduce the chances of this happening to them too. They have developed a process of risk analysis that they term the "What Ifs" and they agonise over gear configurations and how to make them safer. Then they train and train and train until their self-rescue and team rescue skills become instinctive.

Technical divers also talk constantly about safety in scuba diving: at conferences in bars, in dive shops, in Internet chat rooms, on social media. They exchange stories and question techniques and equipment in excruciating detail. When an accident takes place they are hungry for information on how it happened, not out of some ghoulish fascination, but so that they can analyse what took place and compare it to what they do to see if the accident points up any deficiencies in procedures or factors that they had not previously considered.

Debate is a significant feature of this branch of scuba diving. Technical divers are doing exactly what tribal societies do. The Internet dialogues are their campfire chats. There is a constructively paranoid safety culture that pervades technical diving that New Guineans would completely understand.

Sport Divers

Over the years, technical divers have passed on to the mainstream community many innovations in terms of practices and procedures. These include octopus hoses, BCDs and, more recently, side-mount diving. However, unfortunately, they have not passed on their constructive paranoia and this sort of mind-set is significantly lacking in mainstream scuba diving and diver training.

Here is a story that I think illustrates the point perfectly. A friend of mine named Robert was sitting quietly at home one afternoon, when he received a call from a lady who introduced herself as a friend of a friend. She asked him for advice on which dive operator she and her husband should go with if they wanted to dive off Nusa Penida, which, attentive readers will know, is an island off the south coast of Bali, famous for big fish, cool water and strong, unpredictable currents that make it a notorious accident black spot.

Robert asked about their experience and the lady told him that she and her husband were "advanced divers" but had only learned to dive a few weeks earlier. On hearing this, Robert pointed out that diving around Nusa Penida could be tricky and suggested instead that they try some of the wonderful diving in easier conditions off the village of Tulamben on Bali's north east coast. The lady was highly indignant at Robert's implication that she and her husband were "not excellent divers; which we are" and hung up on him.

Two days later, she gratuitously called Robert back to tell him that she and her husband had gone to Nusa Penida and that they had had a perfectly wonderful day's diving. "So there, everything you were telling me was wrong," she said. He did not even know where to start in explaining the various issues involved, so he just told her he was glad she and her husband had enjoyed their dives.

Falling Trees and Sinking Boats

When I heard this tale I was of course immediately reminded of Jared Diamond's stories of falling trees and sinking boats.

The lady and her husband had evidently graduated from their initial diver training with no idea of their limitations as new divers. Their instructor had not taken the time, or perhaps had not had the time, to tell them that many dive sites around the world, even popular ones, are genuinely dangerous for beginners. They were apparently not aware that all new divers, however talented, need to ease themselves gently into the sport and that, no matter how intuitively skilled they may be, it takes a lot of practice to become an "excellent diver." Nobody had taught them to be at all "constructively paranoid" about their diving.

Instead, all the high praise they had received during their training seem to have encouraged them to believe that, having completed the courses and obtained their certification cards, they were now ready to dive anywhere. Indeed, their misplaced confidence was so deeply entrenched that it even induced them to over-ride common sense and dismiss the well-meaning advice of someone who had been introduced to them as a knowledgeable diver.

Just like the young Jared Diamond in the highlands of Papua and on the seas of Raja Ampat, they and many other new divers are unable to assess danger because their training does not arm them with the necessary knowledge. To develop constructive paranoia or any other effective defence mechanisms you need to know a) that there are risks, b) what the risks are and c) how to anticipate, avoid and deal with the risks. But, most importantly, you need someone to inform you of the risks as they will not always be obvious to the uninitiated or inexperienced.

In the world of scuba diving the ones charged with the responsibility for informing new divers of the dangers involved in the sport are the training agencies, via their instructors. However, they often duck the responsibility, as I discuss in more detail in the next chapter "Real Risk Assessment."

Today's beginners' courses rarely incorporate to a sufficient degree concepts such as situational awareness, defensive diving, self-preservation and acceptance of individual responsibility. Yet these are the keys to the development of a constructive paranoia mind set. In the hierarchy of diver training courses such concepts are not adequately addressed until divers begin training at technical or professional levels. This means that divers who never get to these levels remain ill prepared for diving.

Professional Failings

Sites such as Nusa Penida do not only have a poor accident record because of the environmental conditions prevailing there. They are accident black spots also because, not only do many dive centres and mainstream instructors not teach a culture of safety in diving, they do not practice it themselves. Elsewhere in this book, and in the "Drift Diving Disasters" chapter in particular, I quote a number of instances where dive operators acted as if they had no idea of the risks involved in running particular dives and no care at all for the safety of the divers in their charge.

What Can We Do?

In the short term, those of us who work in diving can focus on developing a constructive paranoia culture within our own particular sphere of influence.

We can counsel students on how to spot which dive operators adopt a safety culture and which do not, tell them the right questions to ask and show them the tell-tale signs to look for.

We can work on developing within students a sense of self-preservation and teach them how to take control of their own diving. They need to be able to look at a dive and ask themselves, "am I completely capable of both looking after myself and, if called upon, rescue another diver in the circumstances prevailing in this place and on this day?" Only if the answer is an unqualified "yes," should they go ahead and do the dive.

In the longer term, both individually and as a professional community we can press our training agencies to lay greater emphasis on a culture of dive safety in early diver training programmes. The agencies should also set operational guidelines and standards for their affiliated dive operators to follow, concerning issues such as dive boat safety and cylinder filling. They should ensure that divers are not exposed to situations beyond their experience levels and assign sufficient supervisory staff to all training and diving operations.

However, simply setting guidelines and standards is not enough and this is where these ideas are in danger of falling into the "too difficult" tray. In every field of human endeavour, standards that are set with no enforcement and no penalties for non-compliance are usually ignored. The world of scuba diving is no exception. You cannot rely on the fact that dive operators will always put safety guidelines before commercial or economic considerations, even if the guidelines do make good ethical sense. A good example of this can be found in the chapter "Where's the O2?" Here I discuss the problem of multi-national operators who adopt safe and intelligent procedures regarding the provision of oxygen and staffing in dive tenders in jurisdictions where these are required and enforced but not when they operate in countries that do not have such stringent rules or such effective policing.

So, if performance standards are to make a genuine difference to how scuba diving is taught and conducted, not only do agencies have to offer training and guidance and insist that their members conduct operations to the standards, they also have to actively monitor performance, investigate complaints and discipline members for infractions without fear of losing market share. This requires a genuine will to put diver safety and training quality ahead of commercial gain. It also requires additional manpower and money.

There is an alternative. If training agencies do not work to develop a stronger safety culture within scuba diving, then states may intervene and do it for them, imposing their own procedures and enforcement measures. As I mentioned before in the chapter "The Value of Assistants" and elsewhere, this has already happened in the United Kingdom, where the government has and enforces its own code of practice for scuba diving instructors and dive operators that supersedes all training agency regulations and requirements.

Be professional by

Exercising constructive paranoia in your own diving and when running dive operations.
Promoting a culture of safety in scuba diving as a whole.

24. Real Risk Awareness

In the previous chapter I discussed the relevance to scuba diving of the safety culture practiced by the highland tribes of New Guinea that writer Jared Diamond dubbed "constructive paranoia." An important part of the process was the exchange of stories around the evening campfires that told of accidents or near misses that had befallen people.

Listening to the tales, Diamond learned that the leading causes of accidental death for the New Guinean highlanders were fire, falling trees, getting lost, exposure and infected insect bites and thorn scratches. Thanks to the campfire chats, all New Guineans know the major risks to their survival from an early age and know what to do to give themselves the best chance of avoiding coming to harm.

Diamond was struck by the difference between this and our attitude towards accidents in modern societies. Statistics show that, in our world, the major causes of accidental death are cars and alcohol, used separately and together. New Guineans might assume therefore that the dangers of cars and alcohol would be the things that concerned us most, that they would be frequent topics of conversation and that we would be excessively cautious when we drove cars or drank alcohol.

Of course, generally speaking, this is not the case. On the contrary, surveys show that when asked to rank threats to our safety and survival, the three things people say they are most worried about are plane crashes, terrorism and nuclear accidents, even though these three things combined over the last four decades have killed fewer people than cars or alcohol do in a single year.

Diamond concluded that, unlike the New Guineans, in our modern societies we accept more easily old familiar risks or events that lead "only" to the death of individuals. Conversely we especially fear things beyond our control, events with the potential of killing a lot of people and situations involving new, unfamiliar risks. It seems we do not fear the things we should fear.

The True Risks of Scuba Diving

A similar situation prevails in the context of scuba diving. Many of the false perceptions that non-divers and new divers have of the dangers of diving come from stories fed to them by sensationalist media that highlight tales of shark attacks, running out of "oxygen" or divers that "fail to surface." This last one is a particularly strange phrase but it is often used in relation to scuba diving accidents. Perhaps it is used because it strikes at a fear that there are malicious, mysterious forces down there that prevent a diver coming up from a dive. The real risks of scuba diving such as panic underwater, loss on the surface, over-weighting, over-dependence, diving in ill health and diving beyond your level of training are evidently far too boring for headline writers.

Initial sport diver training tends to shy away from addressing the true risks of scuba diving too, imparting instead the message that the sport is fun and safe, which it is, of course, as long as you aware of and avoid the risks, which are very real! During instructor training, we are even taught to precede every reference to risk with the phrase "in the unlikely event...."

Now, once you describe something as unlikely to happen, no student is going to much take notice of what you say. They have a lot of things on their mind already and do not have enough time or brain RAM available to waste it on something that you have told them will probably not take place. This, of course, is the idea. The training agency does not want students dropping out of class when they get wind of the fact that diving can be dangerous. On the other hand, the training agency doesn't want to be sued for failing to inform a student of potential risks; hence the insistence that instructors use the phrase "in the unlikely event" to precede bad news.

So, in a nutshell, what the instructor and the training agency are really saying with this phrase is "we have to mention the risks of scuba diving so we cannot be sued, but we don't want you to leave the class as we want your money. So we'll make sure we focus on fun and safety until you have finished the class and have paid us in full then if you subsequently discover the risks and decide that diving is not for you that's not our problem. And if you subsequently don't discover the risks and live your diving life in blissful ignorance, then that is great too."

I know I am being cynical and I do not imagine anyone managing a training agency ever actually enunciated such views. But the true nature of corporations is shown by their actions not their words.

Magic Tricks

Not only are instructors and agencies guilty of glossing over the true risks of scuba diving when teaching beginners, for some reason we also tend to over-emphasise dangers that do not actually exist. For example, you will see new divers forget all sorts of things but you will never see one forget to turn the cylinder valve back half a turn so the valve doesn't stick open. Nor will you ever see one forget to rotate the high pressure gauge away from them when they switch their air on, just in case the glass shatters and blinds them. The need to take particular care to avoid these particular "risks" has been seared into their minds in their initial training. But do these things really represent such a danger to a new diver's safety that valuable time should be spent on even mentioning them, let alone reinforcing them so rigorously? Especially when much more important things are passed over or given minimal attention to enable a modern beginners' course to be completed in three days. Magicians might accuse us of using misdirection; focussing an audience's attention on one thing to distract its attention from another.

A genuinely significant threat to the safety of any diver, and one that is not emphasised anywhere near enough in early diver training, is stress-induced panic followed by a rapid ascent to the surface. Beginners' courses typically contain very little guidance or practical exercises on how to manage stress underwater. Even those skills that are designed to teach new divers how to manage potentially stressful incidents are accorded little importance or even just glossed over when a diver has difficulty with them or the instructor cannot be bothered to manage potential problems. The following story illustrates this phenomenon perfectly.

No Mask Diver

A friend of mine had a new girlfriend. The girlfriend was a diver and wanted my friend to learn to dive so they could go on dive trips together. But although he could swim, my friend had a fear of the water. So I was surprised to find out that he had completed a diving course and he and his girlfriend were planning a dive trip. I congratulated him on overcoming his fear of water. "Well," he said, "there were a couple of things I couldn't do." He went on to explain that in the pool sessions he had been unable to fill his mask and clear it without panicking and popping to the surface.

I asked him how he had managed to pass the course and he told me that, after a few failures in the pool (accompanied by some emotional outbursts as I later learned,) the instructor had told him that he should not worry about filling his mask and clearing it, (let alone removing and replacing it.) All he would ever really need to do as a diver was to be able to sniff out any dribbles of water that got into the mask and if he could do that then he would be fine.

My friend of course was delighted to hear this news and when I asked him why he thought new divers were taught how to clear a filled mask or breathe underwater without a mask on, he said that he guessed it was just a challenge thrown in to see how tough they were. I asked him what he thought he would do if he was diving in a current that was strong enough to lift the mask from his face or if his mask strap broke during a dive. What if another diver kicked him with a fin and sent his mask flying?

He looked at me in shock. "Well, that wouldn't happen would it?" I told him all three of those things had happened to me and that none of them were at all life-threatening as long as you did not respond by panicking and shooting straight to the surface from depth holding a lungful of compressed air, in which case you would probably die. By the look on his face I could see that he was thinking if he ever lost his mask that was exactly what he would do.

Like the couple diving Nusa Penida in the previous chapter, my friend is yet another example of the many divers who are allowed to complete their initial training blissfully ignorant and with no realistic idea of the true dangers of scuba diving.

What Must Change

Initial training courses should disabuse new divers of popular misconceptions but also inform them honestly what the real risks of diving are and how to anticipate, avoid and deal with them. Basic skills like air sharing and mask replacement should be clearly introduced as essential survival skills to be learned, rather than random tests to be passed. Someone who cannot master the skills easily should be taught how to master them, not just fed lies and consigned to the whims of fate, as my friend was.

The present disconnect between performing the skills and real-world emergencies must also be removed. A good example of this disconnect is the common practice of teaching air sharing as a purely static drill not involving an out-of-air swim and an air-sharing ascent.

In the real world, every air-sharing emergency that ever took place involved a diver who was low on air or out of air swimming to another diver to share their supply. If both divers survived the incident, then the key to their survival was the fact that they managed to surface together, both breathing from the same cylinder. Therefore the whole sequence from start to finish, from the realisation that one diver has an air supply issue to the point where both divers are floating together at the surface, should be what the divers experience in their training. Furthermore, this should not be practiced just once. The whole sequence should be practiced multiple times so the procedure is burned into the divers' minds and becomes automatic. This ensures that they will instinctively respond correctly if a similar emergency ever strikes for real.

Even a short swim without breathing is sufficiently memorable to reassure a diver that if required they can do it in an emergency and provide a strong inducement to the diver not to stray too far away from the other members of the dive team. The inclusion of an ascent in each training drill reinforces the crucial fact that survival is only assured once both divers have surfaced safely and attained positive buoyancy. Not involving an ascent in every drill can encourage the divers to think that the emergency is over once they start sharing air. In actual fact, of course, not only is the emergency still very much present, the number of people threatened has just doubled. There are now two divers who have a problem instead of one, as both are now breathing from the same cylinder, therefore the amount of time the air remaining in the cylinder will last has just been halved. It is not safe for them to stay at depth with air running out. They have to get out of there in a controlled manner but without delay.

But Me no Buts

To anyone who would use scuba diving's current excellent safety record as an argument for continuing to teach diving as we do now, I would say two things. First, yes, our safety record is good but every year divers still get hurt and lose their lives. We owe it to people coming into the sport to aim at a zero accident rate in scuba diving. Although this may be impossible to achieve, we should nevertheless do everything in our power to try to achieve it and never stop looking at ways of making scuba diving safer and scuba diver training better. This is especially important now when, with divers from populous nations like China, India and Indonesia joining our community, more people than ever are learning to scuba dive and many of these new divers do not have a background of water sports or even much swimming experience. For some, even the concept of going to the beach is a new thing. They cannot be expected to identify the real risks of diving or, to return to the theme of the previous chapter, develop a constructive paranoia mind set on their own.

Second, if we are justified in having a degree of pride in our accident rate, the drop out rate in scuba diving is something we can certainly not be proud of. Industry statistics show that a huge number of people have a scuba experience and then never dive again. Similarly a large percentage of graduates from beginners' courses never do any further training. Taking into account the training limits currently imposed, with beginners limited to a depth of 18 to 21m (60 to 70ft,) this implies that majority of those who do no further training actually do little further diving.

In the chapter, "Sabotaging the Industry from Within," I identify one reason for the high drop out rate. Judging from many conversations with former divers over the years another reason many drop out of the sport is that after completing their training they dive and find that their beginners' course has not given them the level of skill they need. They feel uncomfortable, ill equipped and unsafe. Rather than go back and do more training as the scuba industry might hope, instead they decide that diving is not for them and take up another activity instead. From our point of view, what a waste!

We can make diver training better and focussing on real risk awareness would be a huge step in the right direction.

Be professional by

Teaching divers real risk awareness right from the beginning. Understanding the responsibilities you have towards the students you train.

25. How to Keep your Divers Alive

No matter how long you work in scuba diving, you never get used to the fact that every year you hear of people dying while engaged in this sport we love. The most tragic thing is that the circumstances of the accidents are usually depressingly similar and familiar.

If the deceased is someone you have trained personally then you will be wracked by self-doubt and will constantly search your mind for a reason, something you failed to teach properly, a sign that the diver had failed to grasp some key point. No matter how much friends and colleagues try to reassure you, you will always feel some responsibility. For every deceased diver, there is at least one dive instructor who dies a little inside.

In this chapter, I identify the major causes of sport diver deaths and try to come up with a few recommendations for trying to ensure that the divers you train stay as safe as possible. Rather than focus on the symptoms, such as overweighting, fast ascents or running out of air, I have concentrated instead on the principal issues that lie at the root of most incidents.

Teach Watermanship

As you may have noticed, without their scuba diving gear some divers simply cannot swim and many others do not swim well.

Every diver-training agency has watermanship prerequisites for candidates taking beginners courses in the form of distance swims and timed floats, but evidently there are ways to get around these. Perhaps some instructors think the swims and floats are irrelevant and waste valuable time so they do not ask the students to do them? Maybe they do not supervise the watermanship sessions personally so do not notice when a candidate has difficulty completing the tests?

One might think that a basic human self-preservation instinct would ensure that people learn to swim before they think of learning to dive but, again, this obviously cannot be relied upon.

Over the years, as basic diver training courses have become shorter, the watermanship element has been reduced and more emphasis has been placed on teaching students to handle the equipment. This is a mistake and can tend to produce divers who are over-reliant on their equipment for survival, not only underwater but on the surface too.

In the chapter Masking the Problem, I discuss the state of mind of divers who spend every dive, knowing in the back of their mind that they will bolt for the surface if their mask comes off or floods. Panic is a common reaction when people are in an environment where they are not comfortable and something goes wrong. A diver who cannot swim well will experience similar anxiety. The chances of a diver surviving an emergency are increased substantially if the diver feels at home in the water.

Very few dive instructors are also qualified swimming teachers, a fact that might surprise outsiders. However, a swim coach badge is an excellent additional string to any instructor's bow. It means that if the instructor has a student diver who does not swim well, they have the skills to fix the problem, instead of ignoring it or cancelling the course; both of which are poor alternatives.

With qualified swimming instructors on staff, as well as scuba courses, dive centres can offer general watermanship classes, helping people learn to swim or become more at ease in the water. These classes will give the dive centre a wider customer base and expose more folk to scuba diving. As people become better swimmers and lose any fears they once had, they may see scuba as a natural next step, so the dive centre's core business grows as well.

Keep Them Training

Cynicism often surrounds the concept of further training courses, in that they are widely perceived to be a purely commercial exercise designed to separate divers from their money for just the reward of yet another plastic card at the end of the course.

But further training is important. If someone is diving in conditions and circumstances which they have been trained to deal with, they are much better placed to deal with any curve balls that the gremlins of the sea may throw their way. Divers operating well within their comfort zone are much more relaxed, confident and able to handle emergencies.

Not many divers can acquire all the skills they need just by doing the basic courses then learning by watching. Most people need to be taught to be better and safer divers. Further training will genuinely benefit everyone but, in order to convince your divers of this, you have to find ways to combat the cynicism.

When promoting further training courses, point out exactly what the diver will achieve by taking the class, what specific skills they will acquire and what particular knowledge they will gain. Do not just tell them that after taking the class they will have the rank of XXXX Diver, which, after all, is an artificial designation that is largely meaningless. Point out too that further training courses are also an opportunity for divers to improve their general skills under an instructor's supervision and benefit from the instructor's undivided attention to seek advice and ask questions.

Then, having made these promises, of course you have to deliver and make the further training courses as good as they can possibly be: so good that not only do the divers emerge feeling that they have got their money's worth but they recommend the courses to other divers too.

A number of successful dive centres keep their divers training by organising events at a pool or beach site where no formal courses are being offered but dive professionals are on hand to watch and offer advice as required or requested, as divers go through skill routines or just simply swim around. The dive centres charge a small fee or ask for contributions to cover costs as necessary. There are major benefits to be gained all round from holding such events. The dive centres win in that they keep their customers active and build an excellent reputation for customer care. The divers win from having a no-pressure, low cost, constructive environment in which to hone their skills and become better divers.

Encourage Defensive Diving

The ability to anticipate problems before they occur is something you can teach divers right from the beginning. Some call this defensive diving; technical divers call it a adopting a "what if" approach.

Teach students to consider all the problems that might occur on a dive and ensure they know in advance exactly how they would deal with each problem if it took place. Then, if something goes wrong they will be able to react quickly, correctly and with the minimum of fuss.

Teach them too about the incident pit. Most accidents are an accumulation of events that, unchecked, can take a diver into an increasingly unmanageable situation. This is the incident pit. Once you are in it, it is often too late.

So it is crucial that divers learn to recognise apparently minor events that might lead to more serious situations and have the presence of mind to pause at that point. Then they must decide quickly if the problem can be resolved easily and, if not, have the discipline and courage to call the dive team together and abort the dive, to live to do it again another day.

Take Health Issues Seriously

The diving population in Europe and America is ageing and gaining weight. Heart attack is becoming an increasingly common cause of diver death and the victims of fatal diving incidents are often overweight. Although it is true that our sport does not require that participants should be fit, athletic and built like racing whippets, nevertheless a diver should be in good physiological and physical shape, particularly in order to survive when things go wrong.

Encourage all older divers to follow a basic fitness regime, get regular medical check ups and be aware enough of their limitations not to dive if they become ill, injured, incapacitated or after significant surgery. A history of heart disease should give divers pause to consider whether they should continue diving, given the high number of fatalities where this is cited as a contributing factor.

If it is appropriate, follow the same advice yourself.

As we do more diving we gain in experience, but no matter how much we learn, the laws of nature still apply. As our bodies age they become weaker, we become more susceptible to ailments and our chances of dodging a physiological bullet decrease.

If you feel unwell, don't dive. If you are in a position where you have divemasters and instructors working for you, allow them the luxury of doing the same and create an employment culture wherein they feel comfortable reporting in sick without fear of criticism or stigma.

Sometimes Say "No!"

Diving is not for everyone. Some people have a fear of water; others feel claustrophobic when they don diving equipment. Some folk have nervous conditions that cause them to experience a high degree of anxiety when they put their heads underwater.

Common sense should dictate to such people that diving is not for them and that they should pursue other activities instead. However, rather than heed the warning signs, some see their fears as challenges to be overcome. Peer pressure also comes into play and there are many instances where someone will try to learn to dive despite their fears simply in order to please and spend more time with a diving spouse.

Dive professionals are often guilty of collusion in such cases. We sometimes encourage divers to take training courses when they are not ready or we persist in continuing to teach people who obviously do not have the potential to become safe divers. This does not mean that we should only ever accept the "naturals" on diving courses. After all, there is nothing more rewarding for an instructor than to help someone discover his or her hidden potential. But it is wrong for us to be complicit in another person's self-deception.

Similarly, we should be careful of issuing certifications to those who have been able to accomplish the skills only by depending on an instructor's assistance. It is always hard to withhold certification from someone who has paid for a course but the decision to unleash an incompetent diver onto the diving community should be much harder.

Scuba professionals need to say "No" more often. Sometimes we need to tell students that they are failing. They need to hear from their dive instructor the words that they have probably already been saying to themselves, "diving is a wonderful sport but it is not worth risking your life for. If it is not for you, there are plenty more things you can do which are just as rewarding."

To digress slightly but on a similar note, dive professionals are also occasionally guilty of agreeing to take divers to dive-sites that require advanced skills without asking for evidence of prior experience or in the full knowledge that the sites are beyond the divers' skill levels. We may do this simply for financial reasons. Every business needs money to survive and the argument often runs like this, "if we don't take them there, the dive shop down the beach will take them." Or perhaps we tell ourselves that it does not matter what abilities they have as long as we have the supervisory and rescue skills to make sure they don't come to harm. Sometimes we might say, "Yes" just to be accommodating or because the diver has nice eyes!

Of course, none of these arguments are valid. The correct thing to do is say' "No." By doing this, you take the ethical high ground and play your small part in raising standards, developing a safety culture and making diving safer everywhere.

Bring Divers Back Slowly

A disproportionate number of accidents occur in respect of divers who have taken a few years away from the sport and then try to come back at the same level of diving they were doing before the break. When you are diving regularly and frequently good diving behaviour becomes automatic and correct responses become instinctive. However, these are often forgotten when you have not been in the water for a while.

Encourage divers in these circumstances to spend time with an instructor to go through skills in a pool or shallow water before embarking on a few easy dives first. Don't require them necessarily to do a formal course as this may provoke the same sort of cynicism that I referred to before in regard to further training and may dissuade them from doing anything with you at all. Of course, if they do come to you and ask to go through a formal re-familiarisation course, you would not try to persuade them otherwise.

You can still charge for informal training. In fact, advertising an hourly rate for instructor time is a great way to keep divers learning, breaking the unhelpful industry-wide misconception, encouraged by the training agencies, that if diver training does not come with a new card at the end then somehow it is worthless.

On the contrary, why should the concept of "an end" exist at all in the context of diver training? Surely every diver, whether returning from a break in diving or not, would benefit from an hour or two spent with an instructor every now and then. Many divers fall into bad habits and everyone can use help with their skills from time to time. So why not hire an expert for a couple of hours to review their posture in the water and finning technique or help them perfect their technique for releasing a surface marker buoy underwater? The more opportunity you offer for divers to improve, the safer they will become.

Warn Against Overconfidence

Tragedy does not only strike at new divers: experienced divers also die each year, often through overconfidence. Familiarity with the sport can misguide some into thinking that somehow the laws of physics do not apply to them any more and that they can cut corners and ignore the rules that they preach faithfully to others. Many instructors and divemasters go through this stage during their development and the lucky ones emerge on the other side chastened but wiser. "Trust-me" deep dives and wreck and cave penetrations are common symptoms as are dives at the end of the day on used and nearly empty cylinders.

Be alert for signs of overconfidence in those you train and those you work with and have the courage to step in and say something. With students it is more straightforward; you can always introduce controlled scenarios into the training dives that point up the issue to the diver and the dive team as a whole. I quote an example at the beginning of the chapter "It's not just Beasting" where the diver learned his lesson directly from the dive team and, having set up the scenario, the instructor was not required to intervene further.

Teach Survival

Some divers are alive today having survived potentially fatal experiences not because they are superhuman but because they chose not to give up. Confronted with apparently insurmountable circumstances, something inside them persuaded them to continue in spite of the odds against them. In doing so, they gave themselves the option of survival.

If they had taken the easy way out and just given up, nobody would have known. Their loss would have been mourned and their names would have been entered into the lists of diving fatalities. It is difficult to train someone to adopt a survival attitude but instructors can usefully incorporate survival drills into informal training programmes as I describe also in the chapter "It's not just Beasting."

Be professional by

Teaching watermanship.
Keeping divers in training.
Encouraging defensive diving.
Taking health issues seriously.
Sometimes saying "No."
Bringing divers back slowly.
Warning against over-confidence.
Teaching survival.

26. Drift Diving Disasters

The dive centre had chartered a boat to take five divers and two instructors out to some islands off the south coast of Bali. It was rainy season and, behind the rainclouds, there would be a full moon that night in an area where currents are notoriously strong and unpredictable. However, water conditions seemed manageable, there were other dive boats out on the water and having done one dive without encountering any difficulties, the divers entered the water again for a second dive that was to be a drift dive.

After about 10 minutes underwater, they found that the current was so strong that it was difficult to keep the group together so they ascended early to find that a storm had swept in, surface conditions were now very rough and the rain had reduced visibility to a few metres only.

Gone

Unaware that the divers had surfaced and expecting that the dive would last an hour or so, the boat crew did not pull up their anchor until about 40 minutes after the divers had entered the water. They moved off to look for them in the area they expected them to be. They did not find them. Then night fell and the divers were gone.

A little over 72 hours later, searchers found four of the divers perched on rocks some 20 kilometres away from their original entry point and one of the instructors in the water nearby. The bodies of the remaining diver and the other instructor washed up on shore in the following days.

Not a One-Off

This is not a bizarre one-in-a-million accident. Indeed, it is just the latest in a depressingly similar series of such incidents that have taken place in the same area in recent years.

Just before midnight on 7th July 2012, a fishing boat picked up eight divers adrift in three-metre seas off southern Bali. The divers had begun their third dive of the day late in the afternoon, become separated from their guide and surfaced out of sight of the dive boat, which was then forced to return to port after a very brief search because it did not have night-running lights. The recovery of the divers was completely fortuitous. The fishing boat was not looking for them. In fact, nobody was. A search had been planned but was not due to begin until dawn.

Neither is Bali unusual. Similar stories abound everywhere people dive and there are strong currents.

In 2013 a passing tugboat spotted six scuba divers who had been lost off Tioman, Malaysia. They had spent the previous 21 hours floating in the open sea. In this case, a seventh diver, who had lost contact with the other members of the group early in the dive, had returned to the boat alone and reported them as "missing." The boat went to get help to run a search and, while it was away, the other divers surfaced. By the time the boat came back, the current had taken them away.

Running Drift Dives

In the first example quoted here, the dive operation, boat operator and instructors ran the dive as if they had no idea of the risks of running a drift dive in rainy season, when surface and underwater visibility would be poorer than usual. It was also full moon, when the current would be even stronger than normal. There was no member of the dive operation's staff on board the boat while the divers were in the water and the boat crew failed to exercise any care and attention at all. Nobody was watching for the divers to surface. Nobody had considered what to do if the dive was aborted early.

With a little forethought regarding procedures and personnel, the seven divers would not have been lost that day, it would not have taken three days to find them, they would not have needed the miracle chance that the sea carried them towards some rocks and the two who could not make it onto the rocks would not have lost their lives.

Stories like this and similar tales of near misses that are told wherever divers gather all combine to raise fears of drift diving, which is a shame because dives when a current is running can be the most memorable of a diver's life for all the right reasons.

Running a safe, successful drift dive, indeed any dive, comes down to preparation and communication. While depressingly common, incidents like these are completely avoidable if you assign enough staff to a dive, adopt some basic protocols and use a little affordable technology.

Staff and Procedures

First, no matter if the boat belongs to the dive operation or if it is a charter boat, an experienced and professional member of the dive centre's staff should be on board the boat throughout the dive. This person is the surface supervisor for the dive. This is their sole task. They are not responsible for driving the boat or any other duties.

Before the dive the supervisor discusses with the in-water guides what route they plan to take and what they will do in an emergency. They make sure they have considered all the things that might happen and have a plan for each eventuality. Indeed, the dive operation they are working for should have set procedures for all staff to follow so the dive guides and surface supervisor need only review these and plan for any last minute issues that might have arisen, such as the likelihood of a sudden rainstorm.

Before the boat leaves the dock, the team makes sure that they have enough trained guides for the number of divers in the water. Again, the dive operation should have rules for this, based on typical conditions in the area and the experience of the customers. In the second Bali incident I described earlier, there was only one professional member of staff on the dive with ten divers and a trainee divemaster. In fact, it was the trainee who ended up in charge of the lost group as the guide and two other divers made it back to the boat. This was the trainee's first drift dive ever!

Another major mistake the dive operation made was to conduct a drift dive late in the day when a low sun makes it even more difficult than normal to see heads bobbing in the water. In late afternoon in the tropics, all you can see when you look into the sun is a bright white sea melting seamlessly into a bright white sky. Look in the other direction and the shadows between waves can easily conceal the presence of a floating diver.

As I said, the sole function of surface supervisors is to monitor the dive and their role is as crucial as that of the in-water guides. They watch the bubbles initially to see if the guide is following the plan and, once the divers are en route, they instruct the boat crew to move and accompany the divers from a distance. If difficult water or weather conditions arise, they ask the captain to bring the boat closer. They remain alert and ready to assist if there is a problem, for example if anyone makes an early ascent, and stay on watch until the whole dive team is safely back in the boat.

A Little Affordable Technology

Divers are taught to carry a safety sausage / surface marker buoy (SMB) and noisemakers to help a dive boat find them if they are lost at sea. This advice is now being introduced on beginners' courses although the message does not always get through as it should. I recently came up from a dive a long way from the boat and noticed another diver nearby on the surface with no SMB deployed. I put mine up and he thanked me as the tender boat turned in our direction. I told him he should probably think about getting an SMB of his own. "Oh, I've got one, he said, "it's in my dive bag back on the boat."

Of course, divers should be told to carry surface safety equipment on every dive, whether they expect to use it or not. However, it is sadly futile for them to deploy an SMB or blow a whistle if nobody is there to see or hear it. In the first story above, the divers might well have raised SMBs when they came up but if they did it was pointless because nobody was watching.

In remote backcountry skiing, where avalanches are a risk, everyone is equipped with an avalanche beacon, a device that constantly emits a signal. In the event the skier is buried, the signal helps a rescue team find them. Now, wonderful as it may be to imagine a world in which every diver is required to carry an emergency signalling beacon in the event that they become lost at sea, this is unlikely to happen any time soon.

However, there are simpler and more practical alternatives available right now. A Singapore technical diving instructor friend of mine recently found himself drifting alone in the South China Sea after a series of unusual events. He looked around, saw where he was in relation to the land, pulled out the hand-held VHF marine rescue radio with GPS that he carries on every dive and called the boat to come and pick him up – no drama!

These radios represent without doubt the most significant advance in safety at sea in recent years, not only benefitting divers but surfers, paddlers, fishermen, and sailors too. They cost under US$300 each so, for the average dive operator, an investment of a couple of thousand dollars is all that is required to arm every dive supervisor and in-water guide or instructor with a unit and, by using them intelligently in tandem with the other procedures outlined here, eliminate the risk of losing divers at sea completely. Isn't that what divers should reasonably expect from the people they pay to take them diving?

Other Current Strategies

Not all dives that you run in areas of high current are drift dives. Many wonderful dive sites consist of small islands, submerged pinnacles or shipwrecks in channels where there is fast moving water and where large schools of fish congregate to feed and escape from the current.

To get the timing right for sites like this you need to study any tide tables available as well as be aware of moon phases. A difference of just a few minutes can make the difference between a good dive and a great one. Experience will tell you where the big fish gather when the current starts running and, once you know this, the most important thing is to get your group to the right place. Getting the entry wrong could mean your group misses the site completely and ends up floating in the blue.

Going Down

One common tactic is for the dive boat to position itself directly above the site and have all the divers enter the water together, negatively buoyant, and fin straight down, equalizing furiously as they go. This often results in some divers getting to the site just fine, others arriving panting, confused and with a headache and a few missing the site completely, having delayed their descent. This means that the group is separated from the start and it is already certain that the boat is going to be picking up divers scattered over a wide area for the next hour or so.

A less stressful and far more effective way to get everyone on site together is what is called a "rolling" entry. You choose a point on the surface from which with a normal descent rate the current will carry the divers to the dive site. You mark this descent point with a buoy and then drop all the divers in the water upstream from the buoy. As the divers drift on the surface they can unite with their buddies, give their equipment a quick, final check then, as they approach the buoy, signal and start their descent together.

Coming Back Up

Dives like this often require "blue water' ascents where there is no reference. The boat crew will have a general idea of where you and the group will be ascending as they have been watching your bubbles and know which way the current is running. To help them find you more quickly, to keep the team together and to give everyone a reference, a useful technique is to send up an SMB on a reel from depth. You only need to send up one SMB as long as the group is together. Multiple SMBs sent up together tend to get tangled up. Of course, every diver in the group should still be carrying their own SMB in case they find themselves separated and ascending alone.

The divers then all stay close to the SMB line on ascent and complete their safety stop together before surfacing all in the same place, facilitating an quick and easy pick up.

Drift diving need not inspire fear in divers. If you do have guests that are afraid of getting lost at sea, explain all the steps you are taking to ensure this does not happen. In fact, tell them what you are doing in your general briefings. This will inspire confidence in all your divers and encourage them to buy into your system and stay with the team. Then, when divers gather and discuss drift diving, it may not only be horror stories that are told around the table.

Be professional by

Analysing the risks of drift diving.
Establishing procedures to mitigate the risks.
Acknowledging divers' fears and acting to dispel them.

27. When to Cancel a Dive

As an instructor or dive master you are responsible for many things but your key responsibility is the safety of the divers in your care. Sometimes this means that you have to make difficult and highly unpopular decisions such as cancelling a dive at the last moment if you think the prevailing conditions might be dangerous.

Kate's story

Kate was a divemaster in Hong Kong; it was a beautiful Sunday in early September and she was in charge of a dozen divers who had assembled at the dock for a two-tank boat dive. The sky was blue and the sea was calm. Everyone had turned up early and there was a buzz of conversation about what a great day they were all going to have. They were all Hong Kong residents with busy lives in the city and were excited at the opportunity for a rare day off and out on the water.

However, Kate had been listening to the radio on the drive to work that morning and had heard that a storm was forecast later in the day, coming in from the east. The boat dock was on the east side of Hong Kong and all the dive sites accessible from there were around the small islands even further east.

Kate knew from experience how quickly the weather can change at sea and she was concerned. On arrival at the boat she spoke with the captain, who had not heard the weather report but felt that the good conditions would hold at least through the day. All around, other dive boats were loading their customers and preparing to set off.

Kate took a look at her group of divers. All were quite new to the sport and inexperienced. She could see how excited they were. She thought for a while then gathered everyone around and explained regretfully and sympathetically that, although it seemed that it was going to be a beautiful day now, bad weather was on the way and she felt it would be better for everyone if they cancelled the trip.

The mood turned ugly fast. This was not news the divers had expected. After all, they could see other boats pulling out with happy divers on board. Some accused Kate of cancelling for no other reason than that she wanted to have a day off work; others called the dive centre owner and tried to convince him to over-rule her. He told them it was Kate's call.

Kate stuck to her decision and the divers eventually got back into their cars, disappointed and annoyed. On their way back to the city the sky became dark behind them and heavy drops of rain started bouncing off their windshields. Within an hour a fierce storm was battering Hong Kong. The dive boats that had gone out rolled and pitched back to port through high seas, most with a cargo of very sick customers on board. No-one dived in Hong Kong that day.

To their credit, many of the divers later called to apologise to Kate and thank her for sparing them an unpleasant experience. But the apologies came too late to spare Kate the hurt of their accusations the previous day when all she was doing was trying to make sure they did not come to harm.

Andrew's Story

Andrew was a divemaster working in Thailand for a dive centre that was in financial difficulties. One day the owner told him that he had a group of six divers the next day who wanted to do a wreck dive. All had prepaid and the income from this trip would enable the owner to pay his staff that week.

Everything went fine on the way to the site and the boat tied up to a marker-buoy attached to the wreck while the divers prepared their equipment. As everyone was getting ready Andrew noticed that the line from the buoy to the boat was starting to quiver and that whirlpools were forming in the sea around them. He told the divers that the current seemed to be picking up and that it might be difficult for them to swim to the buoy and the descent line to the wreck. He advised them that it might be better to wait until conditions improved.

The divers were all in their wetsuits by now, sitting fully geared up on the dive deck in the heat of the day. They were not happy to hear this and told Andrew that they did not want to wait. They were ready, they were hot and they had plans for that afternoon so did not want to spend all day on a dive boat.

Andrew relented and instructed the crew to set a surface line from the marker buoy. He told the divers that if they wanted to go now the only way to reach the buoy would be to grab the surface line as they jumped into the water, pull themselves hand over hand to the buoy and then descend along the line to the wreck. But he warned them again that the current was very strong and that he felt it would be better to wait.

They ignored the warning and the spokesman of the group stood up and made his way to the entry point. He dropped in, grabbed the line and held on briefly before the current tore it from his grasp and carried him away. Within seconds he was 100m (330ft) behind the boat and shouting for help.

Andrew asked the other divers to sit down, told the crew to untie the boat and set off to pick up the drifting diver. As the boat pulled away the current pulled the marker buoy under the surface, hiding the wreck's location. With no other wrecks in the area and no option now but to go elsewhere, Andrew took the divers to a sheltered location where they did a reef dive instead.

Later, back at the dive centre, the group asked for a refund on the basis that the promised wreck dive had not been delivered! They blamed Andrew for doing a bad job and, once the group had left, the owner blamed him too.

It's Your Call

You may not be the most powerful or influential person in the company but as the person actually running the dive, the final responsibility is yours, which means that you need to be a decision-maker.

As you can see from the above examples, the decision to cancel a dive is rarely straightforward. It can be influenced by a number of competing factors and often requires a great deal of courage and conviction. Nobody can tell you in advance what decision to make, as the circumstances will always be different.

However, what holds true in every case is that if your first priority is always the safety of your dive group then, no matter if the decision you take turns out to be the correct one or not, you will always know that you acted for the right reasons.

Smart dive centre owners should always support staff who put the well-being of the customers first and, if your boss does not support you, maybe you should be working for a different dive centre!

A Word About Premonition

On rare occasions when you are planning a dive or on the way to the dive site you may find yourself overcome by a powerful feeling of foreboding, a premonition that something will go wrong. If this happens, review the plan and consider your dive group and the prevailing conditions to see if there is anything you may have missed. Run through the dive in your head and, if the negative feelings just will not go away, consider changing the dive site or dive plan for a safer option or even cancel the dive completely. When interviewed after an incident many people report that they felt something bad was going to happen. As you gain more experience in the diving world you develop instincts. Learn to trust these instincts and act upon them.

Be professional by

Having the courage of your convictions.
Always putting the safety and well-being of your divers before everything else.

§5

The State of the Scuba Nation

28. Assuring a Future for Dive Tourism

The future of scuba diving tourism is not completely in our hands. It depends on the good health of the oceans and ensuring the good health of the oceans is a challenge far beyond the scope of the scuba diving industry. Plastic trash, chemical pollution, mining, over-fishing, global warming and coastal development are all threats that we as a relatively small community are powerless to prevent. We can only object and activate to try to influence greater forces to effect change.

When keen scuba diver James Cameron made the movie Avatar, he showed his lead character, Jake Sully, reacting to the wonders of the alien world of Pandora like a diver who goes underwater for the first time. If you have seen the movie, you will have noticed how many of the animals and plants of Pandora are similar to marine life on Earth. The more Sully learns about the Pandoran eco-system, the more he is driven to protect it from the humans who would destroy it. And he succeeds. He leads the Pandorans to victory, the humans are marched back into their space ships and the planet is saved.

If only it were that easy. Cameron created a clever metaphor for man destroying the oceans but his solution exists only in Hollywood fantasy. As scuba diving professionals, we may be similarly driven to protect the world we are uniquely privileged to visit and which we depend on for our livelihood but we do not have a Jake Sully on our side and the inhabitants of the ocean cannot fight back, even with our help.

Of course, this does not mean that we should just stand by and do nothing. And we are far from idle, we support artificial reefs, we activate against sharks fin soup, we conduct beach clean ups and we train divers to "take only pictures and leave only bubbles." However, we can do more! We can widen our focus, address the bigger picture and involve people beyond the diving community. Education and communication are the keys and I do not mean just teaching scuba classes. Let me explain.

I Have a Dream

Over the years, many people have come into the scuba diving industry driven by a dream. This dream is to find a small, sunny corner of the world where the reefs are healthy and where they can set up a little dive resort.

The resort will be built by village craftsmen and designed to leave as small an ecological footprint as possible. Materials will be sourced locally without destruction of either reef or forest. The use of plastics and chemicals will be minimal and sewage and trash will be disposed of responsibly.

People from neighbouring villages will be trained to work in the resort, providing them with employment, twenty-first-century skills and wealth. They will consequently abandon unsustainable practices such as cyanide and dynamite fishing and will have a vested interest in keeping trawlers and long-line fishing boats out of surrounding waters. The ocean will thrive and healthy reefs and plentiful fish stocks will keep happy divers coming, so both the resort owners and local people will thrive.

Compromises

Inevitably, those who follow this dream are confronted by difficult decisions that force them to weigh their good intentions against business interests.

Some of these decisions involve environmental considerations. For example, do you have to provide guests with packaged food and drinks such as pot noodles, cookies, beers and sodas, despite the trash issues these create? Or can you still attract customers if you only offer locally sourced food and fruit juices? Given limited fresh water supplies, do you need to provide a shower and toilet in each room or will guests baulk at having to share bathroom facilities?

But the most crucial decisions involve people. For instance, it takes time to train rural villagers with limited language and hospitality industry skills to become capable managers and dive leaders, so you have to decide if you will wait until the villagers are ready or if you will import your key staff from elsewhere instead.

The easiest and fastest solution is to import. You want to start recovering the costs of setting up the resort as quickly as possible and you rationalise the decision by telling yourself that, over time, you will train local people to replace the imported staff. However, it is unusual to find a dive operation where the senior personnel are actually local. This means that, with the exception of a few low-level workers, the community as a whole does not end up sharing the interests of the dive operation.

No dive centre is an island and failing to involve the wider community closely and completely can have adverse ramifications for you, your business and the marine environment. That part of the dream that involved local people doing things like conspiring with you to ensure thriving reefs is lost.

Here are a few stories that clearly illustrate the problem. All come from Indonesia because this is the region I know best, but the issues are international and similar tales are told worldwide wherever people dive and there are still fish in the sea.

Here Today, Gone Tomorrow

A few years ago, a luxury coastal resort in Indonesia decided to tether a small platform to the seabed 20 kilometres off shore to act as a fish aggregation device (FAD) for a deep-sea sport fishing operation that they were running. The FAD was wildly successful and the guests would catch prize sport fish such as sailfish and wahoo out there. The FAD also attracted a lot of sharks and became an exciting place for both free divers and scuba divers to visit. The resort was very proud of the success of the FAD, which had enhanced the guest experience, created a sustainable fish stock enabling the resort to become self-sufficient in sea food, provided employment for more local boat drivers and guides and embellished the resorts eco tourism credentials. So brochures and press releases were produced and frequent social media updates made sure the news travelled as widely as possible.

One day a fishing boat was seen on the horizon as the hotel dive boat was heading back to base. The next day the sharks had gone. In just one night, the long liner had managed to scoop up every single one. The number of big fish around the FAD also plummeted over the coming months.

A similar episode recently took place in the north of Bali when a local dive centre found an enormous school of barracuda circling at the end of a point that juts out invitingly into the Lombok Straits. That evening, the dive centre owner posted pictures on his Facebook page and held court in a local bar, soliciting divers to join him the following morning to go back to the same site.

He was successful in one respect as he managed to get quite a large group together for the dive trip. However, other people had been listening to him too the previous night. As the divers, crammed into minibuses, were on their way to the beach to board the boats, they passed a fleet of pick up trucks coming in the other direction, laden to the brim with dead barracuda.

Creatures Great and Small

It is not only large animals that are affected. Along Bali's north shore, far away from the tourist hotspots, there are a few sheltered bays where tiny, rare creatures hide. One of these is called Puri Jati. The villagers here are very poor. They do not share in the tourism wealth of the island's south.

Encouraged and assisted by a philanthropic Bali dive centre, a local family has set up a small shaded facility on the beach with fresh water showers, toilets, concrete rinse tanks for gear and cameras and a snack shop. Dive instructors and guides that bring divers here pay a fee for using the facility. The whole set-up is a great example of eco tourism at its best. Local people and professional divers work together for mutual gain and in the interests of both tourists and the marine environment.

Sadly, from time to time, other people along this stretch of coast who do not share in the fees paid by the scuba divers sneak in at night and drag weighted nets along the seabed. Perhaps, they have heard reports of divers coming out of the water with smiles on their faces, and assume the bay is full of fish. It is not. All they dredge up are small octopus and tiny creatures like frogfish, pipefish and rare and exotic types of scorpion fish: hidden treasure for divers but no use at all for feeding hungry families. The day after the nets have passed, the sand that was previously literally crawling with life is a desert.

In all three of these cases, far from protecting marine life, scuba diving activity has the exact opposite effect and results in its destruction. The primary causes are lack of information, education and communication. The dive operations do not have the local coastal communities on board or on side. They have failed to recruit community leaders to their cause; leaders who could explain how dive tourism can benefit everyone in the area. Of course, this is a role that local members of staff at a senior level could perform. That is, if they had some.

The dive operations have not garnered adequate local support or sufficiently involved the community financially, intellectually or emotionally in what they are doing. Therefore, self-interested members of the community have no qualms about sabotaging their efforts. They may not even recognise that what they are doing is sabotage. They may simply be acting opportunistically. An oft-quoted statistic is that a shark is worth $100 (for meat and fins) dead but $1,000,000 (in tourism dollars) alive. For a fisherman, this is not a convincing argument for not killing a shark if the $100 will feed his family for months and if he will not receive even one cent of the value of the shark if he allows it to live.

No Such Thing as Bad Publicity?

In two of the three cases quoted here, publicity was a crucial factor. The operators were sabotaged only after they had made a big noise about what they had found. Some dive operators, on the other hand, try to protect their resources by keeping very quiet, in spite of the fact that this may not be good for business in the short term.

There is a small island in Indonesia that has one dive resort. The island is very difficult to get to and comparatively few divers have been there. The resort has discovered a dive site nearby where hammerhead sharks gather at dive-able depths early in the morning. The water is warm and clear, the reef top magnificent and the hammerheads, both great and scalloped, are fabulous. So far, the resort owners have resisted the temptation to advertise the wonderful things they have on their doorstep.

You have to worry, however, that this may only be a temporary solution. Inevitably, word is going to get out some time and then all that will protect the sharks and the reefs will be whatever local political support the dive operation has managed to build up over the years.

The Biggest Fish of All

Similarly wary, a liveaboard dive operator has been wrestling for years with the dilemma of what to do with a hitherto unknown whale shark population that he has come across. If he announces it and pictures start appearing on social media he will no doubt be inundated with bookings and his bank balance will certainly improve. However, he is aware of what happened the last time whale sharks were "discovered" in Indonesia and wants to avoid a repetition.

In 2010 an article was published simultaneously in a dozen dive publications around the world telling of fishermen on offshore platforms in the deep south of Cenderawasih Bay in Indonesian West Papua who had developed a mutually beneficial relationship with a group of locally resident adolescent whale sharks. The fishing platforms had nets strung beneath them and powerful spotlights attracted baitfish to the platforms and into the nets during the night. The presence of the baitfish seemed to attract the whale sharks, especially at dawn when the nets were full. The fishermen believed that the whale sharks brought them good fortune and, to keep them around, they started feeding them. The whale sharks would surface close to the platforms, mouths agape, and tail-stand almost motionless while the fishermen dropped handfuls of small fish down into their capacious maws.

The news of a spot with guaranteed whale shark sightings brought a rush of liveaboard dive boats into Cenderawasih Bay and scientists too jumped at an almost unique opportunity to study whale shark behaviour. However, shortly after divers started visiting, behaviour began to change, not only on the part of the whale sharks but the fishermen too. Their role in respect of the whale sharks changed from symbiotic partner to theatrical agent. The dawn timing did not suit the visiting scuba divers so the fishermen started working during the day as well as at night.

They would collect the baitfish and start "calling" the whale sharks once the dive boats had paid. They would charge by the hour and dive operators would have to pay both the fishermen and the village who claimed ownership of the bay where the platform was located. When the allotted time had expired the fishermen would stop feeding the whale sharks and the platform would be winched up and hauled away on the motorised outrigger that acts as the platform's central spine when it is in place. Once the bait fish supply stopped, the whale sharks would disappear almost immediately.

As the months passed and more dive boats started to visit, the price charged by both village and fishermen for access to the whale sharks started to rise to the point where it was no longer economically feasible for many dive boats. So, after a year of plenty, the following year saw far fewer visitors and a much lower income. The windfall had been brief. There were reports of conflict between the villagers who had benefitted from the windfall and their less fortunate neighbours and then further reports of disagreement between the village and the fishermen. This led to the establishment of rival platforms competing for the attention of the few liveaboards that were still visiting.

At the time of writing, the situation is confused and the future looks uncertain. It is likely that the outside world may soon move on, the last couple of liveaboards still going there will find other new itineraries to tempt their customers with and the scientists, thinly spread as they are, will turn their attention elsewhere. What could have been a long term scuba tourism operation benefitting both divers and local people will cease, mainly again through lack of understanding and co-operation between dive operators and the coastal community.

Education & Communication

For scuba diving professionals, campaigning on behalf of fish and reefs in blogs and on websites directed at divers may bring you customers but you are preaching to the converted. There are other people closer at hand who can do much more with the message you are delivering. By involving coastal communities and local authorities you can change behaviours that are harmful to the future of scuba diving tourism.

You have to spread the word into the wider world beyond the dive community by involving more local people in your dive operation; training managers, taking on more local guides, converting local dive masters into dive instructors, even taking local people underwater on try-dives. Involve local authorities; get to know the leaders and opinion formers. Talk to them; get them interested. All this activity will build support links and trust with your coastal communities. Their interests and yours can coincide. You just have to show them how.

More Than a Beach Clean Up

I would leave you with an idea to consider to set you on this path. Next time you are running a beach clean up, organise an educational programme in local schools at the same time to tell the children about the consequences of littering and how to reduce waste by recycling and avoiding the use of plastic bags. Then there may be less trash to collect on future beach clean ups. Better still, ask local staff members to run the programme so the children hear the message from people they know and will listen to, not just the crazy foreigners.

Be professional by

Involving local people in your dive operation at all levels.
Spreading the conservation message beyond the dive community.
Focussing your conservation efforts on people, not just fish and reefs.

29. Are Rebreathers the Equipment of the Future?

We are all pretty high tech these days. However, when we dive most of us are still using technology developed in the middle of the last century when most people did not even have a phone in the house and got their news via something called a wireless! Jacques Cousteau and gas engineer Emile Gagnan, who invented the Aqualung in war torn France in the 1940s, would be flattered yet probably horrified that we have not progressed far beyond their invention.

In every other area of our lives we have embraced new technology and other adventure sports have seen huge changes. The canopies used by skydivers, for example, bear no resemblance to those used by their predecessors a generation ago and modern technology has given them previously unimaginable safety features. Yet in the scuba diving world, other than a little tinkering, there has been a strange resistance to moving forward. As far as the equipment we use is concerned the only significant change over the past two decades has been rebreathers and this is still a very small niche market.

Rebreathers seem to offer huge advantages: gas supply is no longer a consideration on most dives, the no decompression dive time is enormous compared to standard open circuit scuba, and the environmental impact of a rebreather diver is also greatly reduced, given the absence of both noise and bubbles. With the advent of mainstream dive industry acceptance and an avalanche of publicity, it may seem that rebreathers have arrived and that if you are a serious diver you just have to get one.

Many think it possible that in today's rebreathers we may be seeing the seeds of the technology that our children will one day use for diving. However, if they have been around in the modern era for over twenty years, why are we not already seeing them everywhere? Are they maybe not as wonderful as the publicity suggests? Are there inherent problems in the way they work?

The Story So Far

Rebreathers are not a new idea: the concept has been around since at least the late 17th Century when Italian Giovanni Borelli first considered the idea of a diver swimming underwater breathing from a bag of air.

The navies of the world have been equipping divers with oxygen rebreathers for shallow underwater assault operations and deep mixed gas units for deep missions for decades and submarines have been fitted with rebreather escape units for almost as long. In the late 1960s, a US company introduced a closed circuit system called the Electrolung and marketed this to sport divers. Early accidents and subsequent legal action ensured that this experiment was short-lived and ensured also that when the idea of rebreathers for sport divers next surfaced it would be driven by European rather than American companies.

This was in the mid 1990s when, encouraged by the development of technical diving and the growing public and industry acceptance of NITROX as a breathing gas, Dräger, a world leader in rebreather technology for military divers, introduced the Atlantis semi-closed rebreather (SCR.) This was heralded as the dawn of a new era for recreational divers.

Semi Closed Rebreathers (SCRs)

SCRs work with a single pre-mixed cylinder of NITROX. An injector allows gas to pass from the cylinder into a bag called a counterlung, from which the diver breathes via a mouthpiece fitted with twin hoses, one for inhalation, one for exhalation. When the diver breathes out into the mouthpiece, his exhaled gas passes through a canister containing sodium hydroxide, which removes the carbon dioxide (CO_2.) The remainder of the exhaled gas then returns to the counterlung ready to be used again, that is "rebreathed." The combination of counterlung, mouthpiece, canister and diver is called the breathing loop. A constant trickle or electronically-controlled injection of fresh gas from the cylinder makes sure the oxygen level in the loop remains breathable.

The diver's lungs are the engine that drives the process. If there is too much gas in the loop, then it is vented into the water via an exhaust valve. If there is not enough gas in the loop then an over-ride valve opens and adds a stream of fresh gas directly from the cylinder, bypassing the injector.

Machines of the Future

In 1995, this sounded very clever and modern and many professionals bought into the technology. Sadly, however, as it turned out, the predictions of a new dawn were wrong. Market demand did not match the media interest. Divers quickly learned that the advertised benefits of these systems did not stand up in practice. They found that an open circuit set of double cylinders gave a diver about the same extended duration as the Atlantis and other similar machines but without the increased cost, risk and complexity. They also discovered that the much-touted silence was interrupted too frequently by the periodic release of a stream of bubbles from the exhaust valve.

So sport divers at that time decided that they really didn't need rebreathers and continued using open circuit scuba like their predecessors.

Closed Circuit Rebreathers (CCRs)

At the same time, other people were developing rebreather systems that were more complex and offered significant advantages. However, they also delivered brand new problems for divers to deal with. These were fully closed–circuit rebreathers (CCRs.) Typically, CCRs have two cylinders, one with oxygen and the other containing a gas to be mixed with the oxygen. This second gas is called the diluent and will either be air, TRIMIX or HELIOX, depending on the depth of the dive to be carried out.

The user pre-sets the desired partial pressure of oxygen (PPO2) that he wishes to maintain during the dive and the rebreather injects little spurts of oxygen into the breathing loop from time to time to maintain the required PPO2. The rebreather's computers constantly adjust the level of the oxygen in the breathing mixture to ensure that the diver is always breathing the optimum gas for the depth he is at, thus extending no decompression times to the maximum or reducing decompression stop times to the minimum.

The diluent gas is only added on descent to maintain the volume of the breathing loop so once CCR divers are at the maximum depth of the dive, unless they lose gas as a result of mask clearing or have lots of ups and downs, the only gas they use is the oxygen that the unit adds to replace the oxygen they have metabolized. This is usually around one litre (.035 cu.ft.) per minute at any depth so a small 4 litre/200bar (30 cu. ft.) oxygen cylinder fitted to a closed circuit rebreather will provide pretty much anyone with enough gas for well over 12 hours.

A Different World!

A CCR can give you quite astonishing performance.   For instance, imagine you are on a dive along a reef wall using air as the diluent gas and a pre-set PO2 of 1.3 ATA. When you are at 30m (100 ft) you will be breathing NITROX 32. You are almost a completely silent observer. You hear the sounds of the sea, parrotfish munching on coral, shrimp crackling, dolphins calling. The natural sounds are punctuated by a slight hiss every few seconds as the rebreather's solenoid opens to allow a tiny amount of oxygen into the loop to replace what you have metabolized. Watch your no decompression time and move gradually shallower. As you ascend, the rebreather will add oxygen to your mix, and the nitrogen level will drop as the breathing loop vents the expanding gas. Swimming at 20m (66ft) you will be breathing NITROX 43, at 10m (33ft) you will be on NITROX 65 and by the time you eventually reach your safety stop at 3m (10ft,) you will be breathing almost 100% O2. A two to three-hour no-decompression dive is easy to achieve. It really is a different world.

For technical divers, this was the Holy Grail they had been looking for. They decided they did need rebreathers and now CCRs have succeeded in dominating the world of technical diving, mainly because of their phenomenal advantages in gas economy. They bring the cost of TRIMIX diving down to manageable levels and enable explorers to undertake dives that would be impossible on open circuit.

The Downside

There is a downside. While simple in concept, CCRs use complex electronics and are expensive to buy. The models technical divers traditionally use are mostly built by specialist boutique companies or by expert and enthusiastic individuals operating out of small workshops so it is usually hard to find maintenance support outside the country where the manufacturer has its headquarters.

CCRs also require a diver to be meticulous in his preparation and constantly focused during the dive. They are highly unforgiving and allow virtually no room for diver inattention. This is mainly because a CCR exposes divers to a couple of insidious threats that can easily sneak up on them.

As I explained earlier, the level of oxygen a diver is breathing on a closed circuit rebreather is controlled by the unit's electronics systems and can fluctuate considerably. Oxygen is essential for life but in too high or too low quantities it is toxic to humans. The first rule of rebreather diving is " Always know your PPO2." Divers must make sure that the oxygen sensors they are using are functioning correctly and always monitor how much oxygen is in their breathing loop. Too much oxygen can cause hyperoxia, whereby the diver's central nervous system short circuits leading to underwater convulsions and, often, death by drowning. Too little oxygen, or hypoxia, causes the central nervous system to shut down completely and the diver blacks out. There are no warning signs.

CO_2 also represents a danger to the rebreather diver. Too much CO_2 in our bodies, a condition known as hypercapnia, results in uncontrolled breathing, makes us confused and disorientated and can be fatal, particularly if the diver is alone. Divers suffering from advanced hypercapnia are unlikely to be able to rescue themselves.

Technical divers may be prepared to deal with these additional risks in return for the cost benefits but most of us want to relax when we dive and we are not inclined towards equipment where the science and preparation time get in the way of the fun or where we have to spend more time watching the machine than watching the fish. This was a key reason why rebreathers did not catch on in mainstream diving in the 1990s.

However, in the second decade of the twenty-first century a series of developments took place that pushed rebreathers back into mainstream limelight.

Industry Acceptance

For any new technology to make significant headway, first the market the technology is aimed at needs to be prepared to accept it. It is useful here to go back a few years and draw a parallel with what happened with NITROX. Before 1995, the only training agencies teaching divers to use NITROX were relatively small boutique outfits like IANTD and ANDI and very few dive centres worldwide offered NITROX fills. It was also hard to find dive computers capable of tracking dives on gas mixtures other than air as these were made only by a couple of companies like Dive Rite and Cochran, which had very small sales and distribution networks.

NITROX diving would have remained a specialist niche market, but in 1995 PADI climbed on board the NITROX wagon, universal public acceptance followed and suddenly all the other mainstream training agencies followed suit. Simultaneously, all the big manufacturers, Suunto, Oceanic, Aqualung and the rest, added NITROX- capable computers to their product lines. This happened so fast that within a couple of years it was hard to find an air-only computer any more.

In 2011 a similar shift seemed to take place when PADI announced a range of rebreather training courses. Before that, only boutique agencies like IANTD and TDI had been teaching divers to use rebreathers and it was still very hard to find dive centres that could provide support for rebreather divers. However, the arrival of PADI's new courses encouraged more dive operations to take a closer interest in the technology and set up rebreather –friendly facilities. It also persuaded major equipment manufacturers to look at developing their own units and add fixed-PPO2 capability to dive computers to help rebreather divers track their decompression status.

The New Wave

New units were designed with an eye to making rebreathers less demanding for the user, tackling some of the drawbacks of earlier systems and reducing the potential for diver error.

They had important features such as: -

1. Cheap reliable pre-packed disposable CO_2 absorbent canisters.

2. Carbon dioxide monitoring technology.

3. Real time decompression calculation.

4. Mask level status displays (reducing the need for divers to monitor their gauges constantly) and

5. Alarm driven switching to open circuit.

The addition of such features meant that the new units did not impose such stringent demands on the diver as previous systems. Simply put, the primary task of monitoring the system was handed over to the electronics and all the user had to do is follow warning messages that would flash when the machine detected it had a problem. This is a similar concept to the way modern cars are designed. You don't have to understand what is happening under the bonnet, you just have to keep to the service schedule and take the car to the garage when a warning light comes on.

These developments were a major step forward in terms of rebreather safety and they did indeed lead to some market expansion. However, the rebreather revolution stalled again. Divers, it seemed, were still not ready to change the way they dived and abandon open circuit diving in any great numbers.

So What Is Still Missing?

Common sense suggests that for any replacement technology to be accepted by the majority of sport divers it must not only cure the problems of diving open circuit, it must also match the advantages. Otherwise divers will simply be exchanging one set of problems for another and it will be hard to convince them that they really need it.

The advantages of open circuit systems are that they are readily available, robust and tolerant of rough handling, resistant to diver neglect, easy to maintain, economical, simple to operate and easy to learn to use. The disadvantages are that they are heavy, uncomfortable, noisy and limit a diver's in-water time.

Even the new rebreathers only cured the noise and in-water time problems. They were still even heavier and more uncomfortable to carry than open circuit systems and did not match any of open circuit's advantages, being expensive, fragile, complicated and time-consuming in terms of preparation and maintenance.

Universal Accessibility

The majority of the world's open-circuit divers do not own their own scuba cylinders. This reluctance to purchase is not a reflection of their commitment to the sport, it just means that they prefer to rent because either they do not want to store and maintain cylinders, they live somewhere where they always have to fly to dive or they have calculated that it makes sound economic sense not to buy.

If a diver has never bought a cylinder, it seems unlikely that they will ever buy a rebreather.

This means that for rebreathers to replace open-circuit systems as a diver's first choice they must become universally accessible. Units need to be cheap enough and reliable enough to persuade dive centres and live-aboards to invest in the new technology and have it available for rent.

For this to happen, there also has to be conformity in design and use. At present, every model is different and certification on one unit does not qualify a diver to use another. I know the comparison is not entirely fair but imagine how difficult it would be for dive operators to offer rental regulators if divers were restricted to using only the brand of regulator they had trained with!

A Vision Of The Future

So the answer to the question, "are rebreathers the equipment of the future?" is, "not yet." However, we are on the right path and it seems likely that one day, and it may be soon, someone, somewhere, will introduce a rebreather or some other technology that fulfils all the practical requirements I listed and captures the imagination of divers as Cousteau did with the Aqualung all those years ago.

Then we will all be able to dive on ultra-silent machines that give us the maximum amount of dive time possible within physical and physiological limits, warn us when there is a problem and advise us exactly what to do to solve the problem.

They will be available everywhere, light, comfortable, fuss-free, easy to set up and intuitive to understand. There will be no need to question whether we really need one of these machines. The answer will be obvious and we will be able finally to consign Cousteau's Aqualung to the museums.

Be professional by

Keeping up to date with developments in the world of rebreathers.
Being alert for other new diving systems that may appear.
Examining fully the benefits and drawbacks before deciding to adopt new technology.

30. The Future of Scuba Diving in a Flat World

In 2005, Pulitzer Prize winner Thomas Friedman wrote his book "The World Is Flat," describing the epoch-defining effects of technological globalisation in the early 21st century. He explained his use of the word "flat" as meaning "equalising." That is, equalising power, knowledge, opportunity and the ability to connect, compete and collaborate.

One consequence of this flattening that Friedman did not cover in the book is the worldwide expansion of scuba diving as a recreational activity. In the last couple of decades, people all over the world in countries where the sport was previously almost completely absent have started scuba diving. Furthermore, new businesses in many of these countries have become significant players in the international scuba diving industry. Planet Scuba is much bigger these days than it was and it is growing fast.

This may come as something of a surprise to readers who live in the scuba diving heartland of the USA and Western Europe where the diving population has aged and the number of new divers has been falling for a while. But in Central and Eastern Europe, Russia, parts of South America and especially in Asia, scuba diving is booming!

It's the Economy

People learn to scuba dive when they have time for leisure and money to spend on leisure activities. In the 1990s, the growth areas for the sport were the so-called tiger economies of Southeast Asia: Singapore, Hong Kong, Malaysia and South Korea. Over the turn of the century, a decade after the Iron Curtain dropped, scuba diving exploded in Russia and former Soviet Bloc countries like Poland, the Czech Republic, Hungary and the Baltic nations, as people embraced new wealth and unprecedented access to free markets and travel.

In the first two decades of this century, the countries where scuba diving has shown most growth, in some cases astronomical growth, are again those where flourishing economies have created a middle class with free time and aspirations to enjoy it. You now meet Chinese, Indian, Brazilian and Mexican divers in resorts and on liveaboards all over the world. The latest arrivals at the scuba banquet are young Indonesians, mostly from the thriving urban centres of Java and Sumatra.

Gear Shifts

From the 1950s right up to the 1990s most scuba diving equipment was manufactured in only a very few countries, the USA, the UK, Australia, France, Italy, Switzerland, Finland and Japan. However, when the forces of globalisation started flattening the world, many manufacturers moved production to China or Taiwan to reduce costs and improve profits.

As new markets for scuba diving opened in Central and Eastern Europe, the established manufacturers were well placed to benefit. Their famous names carried weight and, although they did not adjust their prices for the less affluent new markets they nevertheless dominated, establishing franchises, branches, agencies or subsidiaries in the new regions. However, as the number of divers grew, local businesses evolved, producing equipment at cheaper prices that domestic consumers could better afford, much of it made in the same factories in Taiwan and China that the well-known brands were made. In many cases the products were identical.

Eventually the new manufacturers began to take their businesses internationally to compete with the big names on their own turf. No longer did professionals and businesses from the new scuba nations come to dive shows in the USA and Western Europe only to buy and learn. Now they were coming to show and sell as well.

The process of change continues. Imitating supermarket chains, Internet retailers have started selling "No Name" unbranded equipment manufactured in the same factories that the name brands use and, obviously, this enables them to cut out all the middlemen and sell at bargain basement prices. This not only has an impact on the established industry leaders, it affects companies in the new scuba nations as well. Two years ago, a friend who owns a dive equipment manufacturing company in Central Europe showed me a tough, powerful, lightweight torch that a Chinese factory had made for him. It swiftly became the best selling item in his catalogue but success was short-lived. Within 18 months, almost every manufacturer had similar torches for sale and unbranded models had appeared on the market as well.

Today, with more and more Chinese people becoming scuba divers, the sequence of events that took place in Central Europe is being repeated there. This time, the process is much faster as the domestic production infrastructure already exists in the form of the factories that have been manufacturing equipment for a decade or more for other companies to sell. Now there is a local Chinese market to sell to, the manufacturers are creating new brands of their own. In 2015 there were three major scuba diving trade shows in China and, at the time of writing this book, a search for China diving equipment products on the Alibaba trading website produces over 28,000 results and the website lists over 1,000 Chinese diving equipment suppliers.

Perhaps in response to the new business climate, many of the big names in dive equipment manufacturing are being taken over by large corporations, creating mutually supportive stables of companies, almost as if they are huddling together for warmth as a cold wind of change blows in from the east. One major manufacturer has reacted to the new environment by purchasing an international training agency. This is not the first time that a training agency and a manufacturer have worked together. It is however, the first instance of a single company both recruiting divers and selling them equipment.

Training Trends

As well as the China expos in Hong Kong, Shanghai and Beijing, there are now annual dive shows in Singapore, Tokyo, Okinawa, Taipei, Manila, Jakarta, Kuala Lumpur and Bangkok.

All these events have one thing in common: they are swarming with crowds of young new divers. The ADEX show in Singapore in 2015 reported an attendance of 41,000 people, the majority of them young urban professionals. Compare this with the annual Scuba Show in Long Beach, California, one of the major US consumer shows, which boasts of averaging 10,000 visitors a year. Singapore has a population of 5.4 million, whereas there are 17 million people who live within an hour's drive of Long Beach. In case you may think I have picked a particularly low scoring US show to compare the Singapore figures to, Beneath the Sea in New Jersey attracts 14,000 visitors a year and, over in Europe, the London International Dive Show reports an attendance of just under 12,000.

Just as the established dive equipment producers benefitted from the flattening of the scuba world, so did the major training agencies. In a clear indication of how the fulcrum of scuba diving is moving eastwards, for one US based agency, in 2014, Korea was its largest source of certifications. Ten years earlier the number one market was Central Europe (Poland, Slovakia and the Czech Republic.) Before the year 2000 the top market had always been the USA. For all the training agencies, the flattening of the scuba world meant that their business continued to grow despite the decline in the traditional heartland of the USA and Western Europe.

However, like the manufacturers, developing technologies, expanding markets and customers with different backgrounds and expectations have presented the training agencies with challenges as well as opportunities.

One major challenge has been to adapt training programmes to a changing world while endeavouring to maintain the structures and paradigms that have been in place for over fifty years. The solution in some cases has been to enable the training to be compressed into a shorter period of time. In the 1960s a beginners' scuba diving course ran over several weeks whereas today most people become certified divers in two to four very full days. Yet, the volume of material that an instructor needs to cover in a beginners' course has not changed much at all over the last five decades.

Advances in technology have helped. The theory element of the course used to mean spending days listening to an instructor. With the advent of "audio visual learning" this turned into many hours sitting in a classroom watching videos then listening to an instructor run through the high points. More recently the theory section of the course has mostly involved passing a few leisure hours sitting at home or in a hotel room running through a DVD on a laptop.

Today, someone who wants to learn to dive can study all the relevant theory online, via "e-learning" (the new "audio visual,") long before they show up at the dive centre. They can watch movies of people scuba diving and even study in advance detailed videos showing them how to perform key skills. If they are interested in a particular field of knowledge they can study the topics well beyond the level that anyone ever taught in a scuba classroom. This means that new divers today can be much better prepared than their predecessors. It also means that during the course time, instructors can concentrate on the practical aspects of the sport, spending more time on water skills.

Changes in how people dive have helped too. In the 1960s, the dive travel industry was in its infancy and divers then, once certified, would usually go out and dive together on their own without professional supervision. Nowadays, this is unusual.

Today, most new divers will go on to do all their diving with a dive centre or resort, paying professionals to guide them and help keep them safe. Or else they will dive as part of a club activity, again under supervision. There have been improvements in the reliability of the equipment too. So the reduced time that divers spend earning their certifications has not made scuba diving more dangerous and the statistics bear this out.

Content is King

The second major challenge that the agencies have faced involves the equalisation of access to knowledge and the ability to connect in a flat world. As I mentioned earlier in this book, training agencies are primarily booksellers. Their business is passing on knowledge in return for money. When e-learning was first mooted, all the agencies thought they needed to do was scan the student textbooks onto CDs to replace the books in student packs. Great, they thought, we no longer have to pay for printing and shipping. Our costs will be reduced but we can still charge the same prices. We like this revolution!

That fantasy did not last long! The technology of e learning moved fast and today's sophisticated students expect high quality materials, especially if they have to pay for them. Any online content they pay for needs to be superior to the online content they can consume elsewhere free of charge or they will not perceive that it has value. Spending money just to be able to scroll down a greyscale PDF of the traditional diver manual and passively watch a dull "old world" video is not going to make them feel fulfilled. The content needs to be in their native language too, which is an increasing challenge as new nations and language groups come into the sport. The agencies that understand and meet these expectations are the ones that will survive in the flat world. Those that do not will find themselves competing with and being overtaken by technologically savvy new training agencies, possibly from the new scuba diving nations, that are not saddled with the baggage of previous eras.

One incidental but important issue that the industry is wrestling with is how the fees that a student pays for signing up online to learn to dive can be shared fairly between the agency and the dive centre or instructor that does the practical teaching. The present solution of requiring each student to name the dive centre they will do the practical sessions with when they sign up with the agency online is clumsy. It presents an obstacle to the customer and thus interferes with the selling process. It is also a potential point of conflict between the agency and its sales force, (the dive centres and instructors.) The agencies that find the most elegant solution to this dilemma will be the future market leaders.

Local Heroes

As scuba diving spreads to new markets, opportunities tend to arise for instructors and instructor trainers but unless they have good local language skills the opportunities do not last long. Typically the early adopters in the new nations are good English speakers and, once they have acquired the skills and knowledge, they then start up their own local networks. In 1998 I taught NITROX diving to a group of Koreans, led by a very enthusiastic instructor. A few weeks later the instructor came back to take an Advanced NITROX course and brought with him a printed and bound copy of the NITROX Diver manual in Korean. He now runs one of Korea's largest diver training agencies.

The transition happens more quickly in some countries than others. It costs several thousand dollars to become a dive instructor, wherever you do the course, and, in some countries, this cost, combined with the low salaries earned by dive guides, holds back development of local instructors and allows expatriate instructors to keep their advantage and their jobs. Historically, this has happened in countries where there is a lot of dive tourism like Egypt or Indonesia but where there are not many local divers.

However, as has happened recently in both places, once scuba diving takes off, local instructor networks start to blossom everywhere and dive centres who have invested in local talent benefit accordingly. New stars eventually appear in the new markets too: role models for future generations of divers to follow.

Where Next?

It is not difficult to predict that, if the Chinese economic wave continues to roll, China will become an increasingly significant force in scuba diving equipment production and Chinese divers will come to dominate scuba diving tourism worldwide. If you have a dive centre or resort and you do not start to think about how to attract the Chinese market very soon, you will find yourself behind the curve. By sheer force of numbers, Asian divers in general and Chinese divers in particular will come to influence the direction the scuba diving industry takes in future.

To identify where scuba diving will take off next, watch the business and finance media channels. Look at countries where a newly affluent urban middle class is developing, then watch and wait. Once people graduate to a lifestyle where they have time off and spare money, they rarely have "learn to scuba dive" as their top priority. It takes a while for confidence to develop and for the more basic needs such as health, food, comfort and travel to be taken care of. Then, thoughts turn to having more fun and that is where scuba diving comes in. Sometimes it takes a second generation to rise. The Berlin Wall fell in 1989, yet the first major dive exhibition in Russia was not held until 2003.

Kenya, Peru and the Philippines are three of the fastest-growing economies in the world as I write this book. None currently has a significant domestic population of scuba divers but all three countries have great diving off their shores. If, in ten or fifteen years time, you find yourself sharing dive boats with groups from Kenya, Peru and the Philippines, you heard it here first!

Be professional by

Staying abreast of trends in diving.
Keeping an eye on the state of the scuba nation.

Acknowledgements

I am indebted to a number of people for giving me the inspiration to write Scuba Professional, for sharing their stories with me or for listening patiently while I bounced ideas off them.

Take a bow, Priscilla, Sani, Rashid, Kiwi and Aya from Singapore, Hugh and Seema in Cooperstown, Dom and Lili at Puri Tempo Doeloe, Cindy from Perth, Uwe on Tambora, Jeff also in Perth, Simon and Andrina in Sanur, Kerri and Hergen at Got Muck, Lol and Heike at Rumah Gokong, Ian and Lu in Teignmouth, Jen and Bill in Hong Kong, Harmony and Noriko in Japan, ace journalist Robert Delfs and ace photographer Mike Veitch.

I am also very grateful to Jen, Kristine, John, Peter, Ian and Tim for their contributions to "Alternatives to Instruction."

Spaseeba again to Andrey Bizyukin for another great cover image.

This book would have been much harder to write without the support of David Strike & Sue Crowe at Oztek, Sydney and John Thet, Lunita Mendoza and colleagues at ADEX in Singapore, who gave me the chance to try out some of the material before a live audience. Also Peter and Gunild at X Ray, Barry, Helga and colleagues at DiveLog and Jason and his team at EZDive, who allowed me column space for early drafts of some of the Scuba Professional chapters.

Steve Weinman at Diver Magazine in the UK was the spark for "Remember the Days Before You Were a Diver?" and Judi and

TheDiveTourist.com lit the flame that became "No Dive Centre is an Island."

Finally I would like to record my appreciation for the work of the fine folk at Createspace, Amazon and ACX. I could not have chosen better publishing partners.

About the Author

Simon Pridmore was born in England and brought up around the world, following travelling parents. He went to school in Hereford then studied modern languages at Southampton University. After spells as a teacher in Algeria and Oman, he joined the Royal Hong Kong Police in 1982, transferred to the Hong Kong Civil service in 1992 and developed his writing skills while compiling reports for the Governor and other senior officials. He retired as an Assistant Political Adviser in 1997, shortly before the handover of Hong Kong to the People's Republic of China.

Simon learned to dive in Oman in 1981. He trained with the Sultan's Armed Forces BSAC Dive Club and was drafted by the club to help teach classes almost immediately after graduation as a Class 3 diver because he was a "schoolie." Later he joined PADI as an Instructor then trained with Rob Cason at Fun Dive in Sydney, Australia to become one of the first IANTD Technical Instructor Trainers in Asia.

In 1995 Simon helped Rob in Phuket, Thailand run the first NITROX instructor trainer course in Asia. Later the same year, he and Paul Neilsen of Mandarin Divers in Hong Kong taught one of the first Advanced NITROX Instructor Courses in the region. The course was conducted simultaneously at La Laguna Beach Resort and Captain Greggs in Puerto Galera in the Philippines and among the students was future world depth record holder John Bennett.

In 1996 Simon participated in the first sport rebreather training course in Asia, using ex-Australian Navy Dräger FGTs and completed cave diver and TRIMIX Diver training with Tom Mount in Florida, USA. Then in 1997, he established the first dedicated technical diver training centre in Southeast Asia at Professional Sports Divers in Guam, Micronesia and assisted Tom Mount in Thailand with the first TRIMIX Instructor Course in the region.

The same year, Simon dived with Capt. Billy Deans when he was contracted to carry out deep-water surveys using TRIMIX of the suspected wreck site of the sunken Spanish galleon Nuestra Senora del Pilar off the southern tip of Guam. In 2001, he was one of Kevin Gurr's Pilar Project team, which conducted what was, at the time, the most extensive dive operation ever attempted by sport divers exclusively on closed circuit rebreathers.

Between 1997 and 2003 Simon was licensee of the Micronesia franchise of IANTD, which included facilities in Palau, Truk, Kosrae, Majuro and Bikini. Then from 2003 to 2008 he owned and ran the IANTD franchise in the United Kingdom. While in the UK he also worked as Head of Sales, Marketing & Technical Support for Delta P Technology and Closed Circuit Research Ltd: manufacturers of the Ouroboros and Sentinel Closed Circuit Rebreathers and the VR range of dive computers.

Simon is the author of the best-selling book Scuba Confidential – An Insiders Guide to Becoming a Better Diver and has written hundreds of articles and features on diver training and dive travel for magazines including Sport Diver, Asian Diver, Action Asia, EZDive, X Ray, Dive Log, Asian Geographic and Cathay Pacific Discovery. He has also spoken at dive conferences all over the world.

Today he lives, writes and dives in Bali, Indonesia.

Also by Simon Pridmore

Scuba Confidential - An Insider's Guide to Becoming a Better Diver (Sandsmedia, Indonesia, 2013)

Diving & Snorkeling Guide to Bali (with Tim Rock) (Doubleblue / Mantaray Publishing, USA 2013)

Exploration and Mixed Gas Diving Encyclopaedia (The Tao of Survival Underwater) (with Tom Mount, Joseph Dituri and others) (IANTD, USA, 2008)

Coming Soon

Scuba Fundamental – Start Diving the Right Way

Further Reading

Stress and Performance in Diving by Bachrach and Egstrom (Best Publishing, USA, 1987)

Never Let Them Quit by Bob Clark (Concept Systems, USA 1997)

Technical Diving Encyclopaedia by Tom Mount and others (IANTD, USA, 1998)

Technical Diving from the Bottom Up by Kevin Gurr (Periscope Publishing, UK, 2004)

The World is Flat by Thomas L. Friedman (Farrar, Strauss and Giroux, USA, 2005)

Raising the Dead by Philip Finch (Harper Sport, USA, 2008)

Decompression Illness by John Lippmann (JL Publications, Australia 2011)

The World Until Yesterday by Jared Diamond (Penguin Books, UK, 2013)

Lightning Source UK Ltd.
Milton Keynes UK
UKOW01f1832180915

258901UK00006B/121/P

9 781507 621073